MILLER'S
TOYS & GAMES
Antiques Checklist

Consultant: Hugo Marsh

With contributions from: Olivia Bristol,
Nigel Mynheer and Norman Joplin

General Editors:
Judith and Martin Miller

MILLER'S

MILLER'S ANTIQUES CHECKLIST: TOYS & GAMES

Consultant: Hugo Marsh
With contributions from: Olivia Bristol, Nigel Mynheer and
Norman Joplin

First published in Great Britain in 1995 by Miller's, an imprint of
Reed Consumer Books Limited
Michelin House
81 Fulham Road
London SW3 6RB
and Auckland, Melbourne, Singapore and Toronto

Series Editor	Alison Starling
Editor	Francesca Collin
Executive Art Editor	Larraine Shamwana
Designer	David Worden
Illlustrator	Kuo Kang Chen
Special Photography	Ian Booth, Andy Johnson,
	Martin Norris, Julie Wright
Indexer	Hilary Bird
Production	Heather O'Connell

A CIP catalogue record for this book is available from the British
Library

ISBN 1 85732 273 8

Set in Caslon 540, Caslon 224 bold and Caslon 3 Roman
Origination and printing by Mandarin Offset
Printed in Malaysia

cover picture: *A Britains clockwork lead 'Blondin' cyclist, 1880s*
picture on p 1: *A Märklin Gauge III 'Württemberg' locomotive, c.1914
(shown without non-matching tender)*

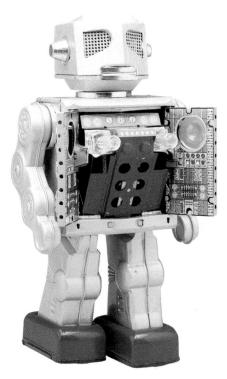

A Horikawa 'Attacking Martian' robot, 1960s

CONTENTS

JAPANESE TOYS 1945-1970

TRAINS 1945-PRESENT

LEAD FIGURES 1945-PRESENT

TINPLATE TOYS 1945-PRESENT

MODERN TOYS 166

SELECTED TOYMAKERS 170

TRAIN GLOSSARY 176

TOYS GLOSSARY 178

BIBLIOGRAPHY 181

WHERE TO VISIT & WHERE TO BUY 182

INDEX 184

PICTURE CREDITS & ACKNOWLEDGMENTS 190

HOW TO USE THIS BOOK

When I first started collecting antiques although there were many informative books on the subject I still felt hesitant when it came to actually buying an antique. What I really wanted to do was interrogate the piece – to find out what it was and whether it was genuine.

The *Toys & Games* Checklist will show you how to assess a piece as an expert would, and provides checklists of questions you should ask before making a purchase. The answer to most (if not all) of the questions should be "yes", but there are always exceptions to the rule: if in doubt, seek expert guidance.

The book covers the range of toys produced in Europe and America from the 18th century to the present day, including trains, games and puzzles, toy soldiers and figures, as well as tinplate, wooden and paper toys. At the back of the book are a bibliography, a comprehensive glossary, a list of principal makers and marks and a useful section on where to buy.

Treat the book as a knowledgeable companion, and soon you will find that antique collecting is a matter of experience, and of knowing how to ask the right questions.

JUDITH MILLER

Each double-page spread looks at items belonging to a particular category of collecting.

The first page shows a carefully chosen representative item of a type that can be found at antiques markets or auction houses (rather than only in museums).

The caption gives the date and dimensions of the piece shown, and a code for the price range of this type of toy.

A checklist of questions gives you the key to recognizing, dating and authenticating pieces of the type shown.

Useful background information about makers is provided.

BRITISH TINP 1945-PRESE

A Tri-ang Minic tinplate, fire engine; made betwe 5 ¼in (13.5 cm) long; value code

Identification Checklist for Triang veh 1945-early 1950s
1. Is the vehicle made from several pa together with metal tabs? (See below.,
2. Does it have black rubber tyres? (M War Two vehicles have white tyres.)
3. Does it have die-cast hubs? (These expensive to produce than pre-war ch
4. Is it similar in design to a pre-war v
5. Does it have original paint work?
6. Is it well-made?

Triang (1919-present)
Triang was founded in 1919 as an offshoot of the Lines family toy-making business. In the 1930s they started to produce a range of small transport vehicles calling them the Minic series. Unlike many companies which collapsed during World War Two when their factories were turned over to arms production, Triang survived and continued to make Minic toys until the mid-1960s.

Main features
This colourful fire-engine has many features typical of post-war Minic vehicles:
* more brightly coloured than the pre-war versions (the range

of models i
* designed
accurate to
rated in the
railway lay-
* popular w
engines, pr
and buses,
tary vehicle
* good-qua
Some vehi
pre-1939, e
during the
after 1945.
* clockwor
models we
and-go flyw
* a colourf
box. Some
boxed pres

162

Makers' marks are explained.

The second page shows you what details to look for.

TINPLATE TOYS 1945-PRESENT

Marks
Triang always marked toys with a gold-coloured embossed triangle (representing the partnership of the three Line brothers).

Buying British
After the end of World War Two, there was a growing enthusiasm for buying British products. After the dominance of German toys in the 1930s, British toys saw a upsurge in popularity and became a symbol of national patriotism.
Typical of this attitude is the advertisement hoarding 'Thanks for buying British' on this bus (below) by Wells (1919-1965), often known as Wells O' London. Notice how it is marked with the name 'National Service', a state-run bus company.

* Period details are always very appealing – notice the pipe smoker on the upper deck and how many people are wearing hats!

Packaging
Paper shortages after the war meant that packaging was often basic, as with the box for the toy lorry (below) by Chad Valley (1897-1979), where a new label has been pasted over a box from another model.
Chad Valley had established a strong reputation for tinplate toys during the 1930s, but this clock-work buffet car made c.1951 shows a marked decline in the quality and detail of lithography.

Tinplate decline
This tinplate policeman (below) by Mettoy (1936-82) is a vivid example of the decline in quality of British tinplate toys from the 1950s onwards.
* The British policeman (below) has a simple mechanism, he simply sways from side to side, and is fairly low in value.

*Mettoy was founded in Britain 1933 by Philip Ullman, head of the German company, Tipp & Co, after he had to leave Germany. In the 1960s they introduced the Corgi range of diecast vehicles (see page 118).

Plastic toys
By the 1960s plastic toys had superseded tinplate. Inexpensive to produce, durable and safe, plastic toys were frowned upon by some adults but were instantly popular with children.

Collecting
Television became increasingly important to children by the late 1950s and toy makers produced many plastic TV-related toys. Often of a high quality, many are highly collectable, such as the plastic 'Stingray' (above) by Lincoln International made c.1963.

163

Further photographs show:
* items in a similar style by other toymakers
* similar, but perhaps less valuable toys that may be mistaken for the more collectable type
* variations on the toy in the main picture.

Hints and tips help you to assess factors that affect value, for example condition and availability.

The codes are as follows:

A £10,000+ ($15,000+)
B £5-10,000 ($7,500-15,000)
C £2-5,000 ($3-7,500)
D £1-2,000 ($1,500-3,000)

E £500-1,000 ($750-1,500)
F £200-500 ($300-750)
G £100-200 ($150-300)
H under £100 ($150)

INTRODUCTION

The desire to play is as old as childhood itself. The unique power of the human mind has always given children the ability to create their own special world, even if their earliest playthings were mud and stones. As civilisation developed, toys tended to reflect the adult world in miniature.

However, not until the various benefits of the Industrial Revolution in the 19thC was it was possible to create a mass market dedicated to the needs of children. As toymaking developed as an industry, every country or region had its speciality: tinplate in Germany; painted wood in central Europe and Russia; paper and wood in Britain; and cast iron in America. With increasing international trade, export markets grew rapidly too. Germany took the lead as the world's main toy exporter from the mid-19thC until the 1950s, when it was superseded by Japan and later America and Far Eastern countries, which are still world leaders today.

For over a hundred years toys have been manufactured as commodities, widely available and for the most part, easily affordable. So, why has the market for old toys and games recently turned into a multi-million pound business? Until the 1960s, manufacturers saw better quality and design as the key to success, rather than trying to create potential antiques, criteria which have been almost replaced today by saturation marketing and response to the latest fashions.

The earliest toy collectors were often people who simply enjoyed their toys, lead soldiers or trains. Some pioneers started collecting as early as the 1930s, but it was in the 1950s that interest really started to take off, led by enthusiasts who took the opportunity to buy cast-off 'rubbish' for a pittance. These collectors were the first people to be aware of the supreme quality of toys from the 'Golden Age' of German toy production, between 1900 and 1914, and bought and exchanged toys with pure excitement, without any reference books or specialised information, and without money-making motivation.

Train collectors were doing the same. Fascinated by actual mainline trains, collectors could find top-quality toy locomotives, such as the Hornby Series 'Princess Elizabeth' for only a few pounds. In Britain, the Sussex Toy and Model Museum in Brighton and the London Toy Museum demonstrate what far-sighted individuals could amass, starting in the 1950s. By the 1960s these pioneers started to publish books about their interests, establish enthusiasts' clubs and hold fairs, while the major auction houses began to hold specialist auctions in toys. A further wave of new books on toys in the 1970s coincided with the first boom for nostalgia, when many more people began to buy Victorian and Edwardian toys for the first time.

Today, the toy market has matured. The raw enthusiasm is still there, but now money and fashion play a more important part. It is now apparent that there are many 'Golden Ages' of toy production, such as Märklin and Hornby '0'

Gauge between 1930 and 1940, Japanese space toys and robots in the 1950s and early 1960s and Dinky Toys and Hornby-Dublo trains from 1958-1964.

Furthermore, collectors are now assaulted by huge numbers of specialist books and magazines and the prospect of future collecting fields, such as Action Man toys, Star Wars memorabilia, McDonalds' premiums, EFE diecast buses and Lledo vans. So, where should a collector start?

Thoughtful collectors try to set themselves strict parameters. They realise that almost no one has an open cheque book, so they concentrate on one particular make or type, and then aim to find the best possible toys in that area, mint and boxed if appropriate. Collectors should be their own sternest critic: look at a toy objectively, and try not to be swayed by the fear that another will never turn up. If forced to accept a rarity in poor condition, try always to trade up, refining the collection ruthlessly.

But, above all, collecting should never be regarded as an investment: despite newspaper headlines, the market is now stable, and it is better that it should remain so, rather than grow again suddenly. A static collection produces no financial income, but it does provide the income of pleasure, which is far more important.

The toy market is now so large and diverse that it may appear overwhelming to a new collector, but it can be approached from several angles. First, do homework - read and understand as much as possible about the subject, including the specialist weekly and monthly magazines, as well as books. This is no substitute for actually handling items, but background reading is an important part of the groundwork. Second, go to any of the huge number of weekly toy fairs and swapmeets to meet collectors, dealers and enthusiasts and to check on quality, prices and availability. Third, visit dealers' shops: reputable dealers can find almost anything anywhere and are some of the best allies a collector can have, with their wide-ranging knowledge.

A parallel source is the auction house. In Britain and North America, there are numerous local and specialised auctions, as well as regular specialised sales at major auction houses. Good auction house catalogues give detailed condition statements on items in the sale, often with illustrations, and aim to evaluate all pieces objectively – to be the eyes of those who cannot attend an auction, as many buyers bid without viewing the sale – and provide an unrivalled source of fresh and exciting items.

If attending an auction for the first time, remember to have a clear idea of the top price you wish to pay, don't feel overawed by the occasion and don't forget to add buyer's premium (usually between 10 and 15 percent).

Collecting toys and games should be enormous fun; it is infinitely satisfying and a wonderful way to retain the magic of childhood.

HUGO MARSH

BASICS

Certain features, common to all types of toys, should be taken into account when assessing authenticity and value. These six pages highlight the basic elements which apply to many of the toys and games mentioned in this book.

MEDIA

Toys are classified by the medium from which they are made, such as wood, composition, tinplate or paper.

Cast-iron

Cast-iron was predominantly used by American toymakers in the 19thC for the manufacture of all types of toys, especially money banks.

Beware of poor-quality Taiwanese fakes that have flooded the market over the past 20 years. These are identifiable by the poor fit of many components and fettling of edges, modern screws and springs and badly operating features.

In addition, reproductions are often slightly smaller than the original, and paintwork is acidic in colour and thinly applied, as opposed to the thickly applied colours of the original.

Diecast metal

Magnesium/zinc alloy which can be easily moulded (see under **Technique** below).

Celluloid, rubber and plastic

Celluloid and plastic are materials closely associated with 20thC toys from the Far East, although they originated in America in the 19thC. Celluloid, initially the trade name for a mixture of nitro cellulose (or Pyroxylin) and powdered camphor, was patented in the United States in 1869 by the Hyatt Brothers in their quest for a substance suitable for making billiard balls.

Celluloid toys were first made in large quanties in the 1940s and by Far Eastern toymakers and by the 1950s they had also developed the use of plastic. European and American toymakers quickly followed this lead and by the late 1960s over half the toys produced worldwide were made in plastic.

Early rubber components were made of natural material, becoming synthetic by the mid-1950s,

allowing manufacture of such items as 'Bendy Toys'.

Most rubber materials have a poor survival rate. Fortunately their purpose was usually as an accessory. Edwardian cars are rarely found with original white tyres; even Dinky, Minic and Britains toys from the 1940s and 1950s suffer from congealed tyres and tracks, so watch out for replacements.

Celluloid toys have rarely survived from the 19thC, as they are extremly fragile and ephemeral in nature. Celluloid's most famous use was in pre-and post-war Japanese toys, with Disney associated items particularly sought after.

Modern synthetic plastics came into general use in the early 1950s, mainly in the toy soldier industry. Far from indestructible, plastic becomes both brittle and sticky with age. If it gives off a sweet smell, this is a sign of potential damage.

Composition

From the late 19thC toymakers began to produce toys from composition. This material comprises kaolin (white china clay), sawdust and glue and was used in particular to make a variety of toy figures by the German toymakers, Elastolin and Lineol.

Composition figures tend to crack with age, particularly if the wire armature has rusted slightly. As it is soft, rough handling tends to flake paint and detail, which reduces the toy's value.

Lead

'Flat' lead figures first appeared as 'spin-offs' from engraving in Germany in the 18thC, with 'solids' (solid-cast figures) popular in the 19thC. British toymaker William Britain perfected the hollow-cast process in 1893 (see below) and the British developed a world domination in this field, right up to and including the present day.

Lead was also used for cheap 'Penny Toys', 'slush-cast toys (see below) hollow-cast vehicles and also for early Dinky Toys.

Although durable, this softness makes paint and limb damage all too easy; damp, acidic conditions create 'lead rot', causing terminal damage to a collection.

Paper and paper and fabric

Paper has been used for many centuries to make toys. It is used either on its own, for example to make scraps for scrapbooks in the 19thC or card for toy theatres, board games and puzzles or it is combined with wood to produce toys such as toy ships, figures and buildings. In both cases the paper has usually been either hand-painted or printed with a design.

These media are even harder to conserve than wood (below) and suffer from insect damage, rotting and fading caused by the sunlight, as well as acid decay. Ironically, paper manufactured before 1860 is far more likely to survive in good condition, as it will usually be 'rag' paper with a high alkaline fibre content.

With the advent of commercially-harvested forests, wood pulp paper became widely used.

It is highly acidic and yellows and crumbles rapidly, making conservation very difficult and expensive, as the pH value has to be altered. This problem particularly applies to games, especially boxes and instructions.

Look out for original clothing on toys by Stevens & Brown, Crandall, Ives, Fernand Martin and Schuco. Originality can make a great difference to a piece.

Papier-mâché

This material was sometimes used instead of wood for toys such as skittles in the 19thC, as it enabled complicated forms to be produced in large quantities much more easily and without the need for hand-carving. However, it is more vulnerable to damage and condition is therefore an important factor.

Painted steel

Painted steel was typically used in America in place of tinplate to make large-scale, usually rather crude vehicles, and still is today. It was also used to make large-scale Triang toys c.1960. Neither category is very collectable in Britain as yet.

Tinplate

Made from tinplated iron or steel, these types of toys were produced in increasing quantities from the mid-19thC. Until then most toys were wooden and generally home-produced.

When tinned iron from South Wales became widely available, it was mainly used for simple, practical containers and decorative wares, known as 'tole peint'.

Tinplate, as we know it, was not widely used until the advent of tinned sheet steel in the latter part of the 19thC. Apart from revolutionising the food industry, tin also gave a huge resource to toy manufacturers.

The thin coating of tin that helped food survive for months has also ensured the survival of magnificent toys.

It is also worth remembering that tinplate toys were not always exclusively made of tinplate, but often included parts made from other materials, such as cloth, wood, diecast, alloys, paper, glass and all types of plastic, from celluloid to vinyl.

In the 1830s the first tinplate toy factories opened in America. These catered largely for the domestic market, with only few exports abroad. The toys were only produced for a short period compared with those that were made in Europe.

Large-scale production by the German industry for worldwide distribution was not achieved until the last years of the 19thC and, with only a few notable exceptions, the mass production of German tinplate toys did not prosper following the end of World War II.

Wood

Wood, along with pottery and bronze, was one of the earliest materials used to make toys. A readily available and inexpensive commodity, there are records showing that wood was hand-carved into all types of play things, such as toy carts and figures, by Middle Eastern people from the Early Dynastic period of 3100-2686 B.C. Wood continued to be widely used until the mid-19thC when tinplate superseded it. However, many traditional wooden toys are still produced today.

Although probably the most widely used material in toy manufacture, its fragility means that relatively few good toys survive in this medium. Prone to rot and damage, this weakness makes the discovery of fine late 19thC American wooden toys in good condition very exciting. Other popular surviving wooden toys include bow rocker or safety rocking horses, velocipedes (small tricycles with horses' heads) and prams.

Original British horses are made from laminated blocks of pine, neatly carved and gessoed, showing a fine degree of muscle and tension. Beware of crude fakes from the Philippines, identifiable by the typical use of hardwoods, deep musculature and rigid poses.

Also popular, but less valuable, are pull-along carts, lorries, ice cream carts and skittles. These toys were usually made from painted soft woods or mahogany.

TECHNIQUE

Toys have been made in a wide variety of ways from simple toys made at home to carved wooden toys produced by craftsmen and modern day plastic moulding using sophisticated machines and robots.

Carving

It is often difficult to distinguish between home-made and factory-made wooden toys. Nevertheless, a number of important toy manufacturers made products that are generally distinctive and easily recognised. Germany, and in particular the Erzgebirge region in Saxony, was pre-eminent in the production of attractive wooden toys, and many were made, mostly for export.

Another important distinction can be drawn between American wooden toys and European ones. American toys are characterized by the application of lithographed paper to flat surfaces, cut to shape. European toys are usually fully carved or turned and any decoration is painted directly on to the wood.

This means that American toys are much more difficult to restore and so the condition in which a piece has survived is much more important than it is for European wooden toys.

The 19thC American toymakers, Charles M. Crandall and his cousin Jesse A. Crandall patented in 1867 a unique tongue-and-groove system which allowed blocks to be interlocked.

They went on to apply the principle to wooden figures, the heads and limbs of which were interchangeable, so that many different movements could be made. Their methods were frequently copied by other makers.

Ring method

Another successful technique for carving wood was the ring method. The hand-carving of animals for farmyards and arks was a laborious process which was superseded in the late 19thC by the ring method technique. A large circle of wood was turned so as to produce a large groove (representing the space under the belly of the animal) and sometimes a second groove for the nape of the neck. The animals were then cut from the ring into slices. The legs were separated and then details, such as ears and horns were carved in. This method produced an unrealistic uniformity; horses, dogs, sheep and antelope often have the same basic shape.

Whereas early hand-carved animals are fully rounded with fine detail, the ring method produced animals which taper (usually to the front).

Cast-iron moulding

Cast-iron toys were made by pouring molten iron into moulds consisting of wet sand (contained in a frame), into which designs had been impressed from wooden patterns. Typically, a toy was cast in several parts and the parts then assembled by iron pins, bolts or rivets. The sand-casting method allowed for a variety of three-dimensional effects and detailing.

Diecast

Diecast toys are made from metal cast under pressure in a mould. A simple form was used first in France between 1900 and 1920 to produce small vehicles (approximately 1½in (4cm) long). Lead was originally used as the main material in the diecast process, but by the 1930s, owing to fears about its safety, it had been replaced with mazac, a magnesium zinc alloy first used by Tootsie Toys (see p.110) and still used today.

Hollow-cast

In Britain and America, the most popular method of manufacturing toy figures from the late 19thC until the 1950s was hollow-casting – a process perfected by the toy figure maker, William Britain Junior, in 1893.

Hollow-casting involves pouring a molten mixture of lead, tin and antimony into an engraved mould, so that a skin forms on the inside of the mould. As the antimony cools, it expands and gives fine detail to the casting without the support of solid metal. The bulk of the alloy is poured out while still molten, which is why hollow-cast figures have holes in their heads or feet.

These figures use less metal than solid figures and are thus less expensive to make and to transport.

Solid cast
The solid-cast technique was used by early figure manufacturers, such as Lucotte, Mignot and Heyde. Lucotte is distinguished from the other makers as they cast the body and head of the figure individually and inserted the head into the body by using a plug on the underside of the head of the toy figure.

Painted tinplate
German factories started making a wide variety of toys based on systemised production. With presses to shape, emboss and stamp out components, skilled metal smiths soldered the parts into boats, carriages and trains. Painting was done with simple but thorough care by hand, in a rich, almost enamelled finish. This was the style still used by Märklin for their premier products until around 1930, although most other makers had ceased to use it at least 15 years earlier.

The Nuremberg style, as used by Bing from the 1890s onwards, relied on much lighter gauge tinplate, allowing for more impressed detail, with a thinner paint style. Instead of being soldered, pieces were tabbed together, U-shaped tabs on one piece protruding through a corresponding slot in another piece then folded over. This method permitted rapid mass production.

Later refinements included spraying, used for Hornby trains from 1920 onwards, followed by oven-baking to produce a durable and lustrous finish. A similar process was used for Dinky Toy production, after the introduction of mazac alloy models in 1934.

Companies such as Triang used only a simple dipping process for their Minic range between 1935 and 1963. As painted tinplate grew simpler and cruder in post-war Europe, so the Japanese reached a peak of production between 1955 and 1965.

Lithographed tinplate
Early decorative printing on tin used the transfer process, already used with ceramics from the 18thC. Ink was carried on a paper membrane, then transferred on to the tin surfaces and baked. This process only worked for simple shapes, and was not durable. In 1877 Bryant & May acquired the sole rights for offset lithography, a new process invented in 1875 whereby a design was broken down into separate plates in registration, building up to a bright colour image. By 1903, in the hands of German makers and the advent of the rotary process, lithography dominated the Nuremberg manufacturers, allowing both intricate detail and speed of production. It then became the most widely accepted method of toy production in America, Europe and Japan for the next 70 years.

Tinplate restoration and fakes
Edwardian toy cars, trains and boats were made for hard use. Unfortunately, the unscrupulous have realised that very rich collectors will not pay premium sums for playworn toys. For this reason, if buying in this field, it is wisest to assume that an old toy or train has been restored unless it can be proven to the contrary.

Fortunately, complete replicas designed to deceive are rarely found, but important components can be identified as replacements. Unfortunately, this is also true for relatively modern space toys and many diecasts. The famous 1956 Nomura 'Robbie the Robot' and associated 'Robbie Space Patrol' (see p.136) are both available as good-quality reproductions, which has affected the prices of the originals. Fortunately, the lithography is not quite as clear as on the originals and, under close inspection, the boxes reveal copies of the small creases on the original box used for duplication.

OTHER FEATURES

Boxes
For many collectors, a mint and boxed toy is the ultimate goal. This is particularly true of diecast toys, where a box can add anywhere between 10 and 2,000 per cent to the value. It is also vital to the value of lead soldiers, which should preferably be

strung on to the original insert card as well. This is also true of Hornby '0' Gauge trains and Hornby-Dublo, while Bassett-Lowke collectors care very little for boxes.

Paintwork

The presence of original paintwork is of paramount importance for the value of any toy, whether tinplate, wooden or diecast. Increasingly, collectors are aiming to fill awkward gaps in mature collections, so will accept only the best. Even perfect condition alone cannot be rivalled by the lustrous gleam of toys that have been stored in darkness for 50 years or more. With Dinky Toys, colour shade can make a vast difference to value, sometimes up to 500 per cent.

Motors

Märklin motors tend to be broader and more powerful than motors on other makers' toys, particularly their boats. Before tampering with them, remember that a wound spring is very dangerous. It is also unwise to run live steam models or early Alternating Current electric locomotives. Old variable resistors and transformers usually fall far short of today's standards and can cause death and destruction; if in doubt seek the advice of a qualified restorer or collector.

Identifying features

Most toys made after 1920 have some form of identification on them, usually a trademark (see **Makers' Marks**) or country of origin. Exceptions include some toy soldiers and inexpensive 1940s British diecast motor cars. Japanese space toys or their boxes are usually marked, but so little is known about the companies involved that the information is still academic.

More difficult to identify are pre-1914 toys by German makers, including Bing and Märklin. Much can be judged on stylistic grounds, but special features can be observed too. Märklin cars and trains, for example, have a bolder, plainer and more massive look than Bing or Carette, using thicker tinplate, with less stamped curves. Car wheels tend to be made of tinplate, oversized and of the artillery pattern (with convexed spokes).

Wing supports tend to be plain on Bing and Märklin cars, but are of waisted form on most Carette cars. Carette's lithographed cars are not usually marked, but their fine quality sets them apart from lesser makers, such as Eberl and Fischer. Carette did mark their railway stock for Bassett-Lowke from about 1912.

Bing lithography always incorporated their mark, as do most of their painted cars and boats. Günthermann and Issmayer lithography tends to be very shiny, with bright and clearly lacquered gold lining; Günthermann cars sometimes incorporate fine painted tinplate figures.

Restoration

In general, the less restoration a toy undergoes, the better. However, certain type of toys are susceptible to particular problems, and may require limited restoration to prevent them from deteriorating further. Remember that bad restoration can cause irreversible damage and dramatically reduce the value of a toy. If in doubt, it is always best to check with a specialist dealer, auction house or museum first, particularly when dealing with costly toys or trains.

Conservation

Toys and trains should only be gently dusted. preferably using a very soft brush. Cleaning should be undertaken with water and a minute quantity of detergent. Avoid commercial polishers and colour restorers.

Display

Toys and trains can be displayed in a multitude of equally effective ways, but is is always important to choose a method of display which will be appropriate to your environment.

Although toys and trains need to be protected from hazards, such as direct sunlight and damp, many people display their collections throughout their homes, perhaps surrounded by suitable accessories.

If you have young children or pets, your collection of toys would probably be safer locked in a cabinet out of harm's way.

It is worth remembering too that if the toy or train comes with an original box to always keep this safe, even if you do not wish to display it, as it can add great value to the piece.

MAJOR TOYMAKERS

MAKER	COUNTRY	DATES
Tinplate toys		
Alps Shoji	Japan	c.1950-present
Bing	Germany	1879-1933
George Brown	USA	1856-1880
Burnett	Britain	1905-1939
Carette	Germany	1886-1917
Chad Valley	Britain	1823-present
Distler	Germany	1890-1960
Francis Field & Francis	USA	1838-1870s
J.M. Fallows & Son	USA	1874-1900
Ives	USA	1868-1928
Lehmann	Germany	1881-present
Lines Bros. /Triang	Britain	1910-1971
Märklin	Germany	1859-present
Fernand Martin	France	1876-1912
Masudaya	Japan	c.1940s-present
Nomura	Japan	c.1920-present
Ernst Plank	Germany	1866-1934
Cast-iron and banks		
Carpenter	USA	1894-c.1945
Hubley	USA	1894-1940s
Kyser & Rex	USA	c.1875-1900
C.G. Shepard	USA	c.1865-c.1895
Stevens & Brown	USA	1843-c.1930
Wood		
R. Bliss	USA	c.1835-c.1895
W.S.Reed	USA	1876-1897
Milton Bradley	USA	1860-present
Albert Schönhut	USA	1872-c.1935
Trains		
Lionel	USA	1900-present
Hornby	Britain	1920-present
Rossignol	France	c.1868-1962
Radiguet	France	1875-1910
Lead figures		
Britains	Britain	1860-present
Georg Heyde	Germany	c.1845-1949
Charbens	Britain	1920-1955
Elastolin	Germany	1910-1984
Grey Iron	USA	1920-1939
John Hill & Co.	Britain	1898-1959
Herald Miniatures	Britain	1950-1983
Lineol	Germany	1920-c.1941
Lucotte	France	1760-1825
C.B.G. Mignot	France	1825-1993
Pixyland	Britain	1922-1932
Taylor & Barrett	Britain	1920-1939
Diecasts		
Corgi	Britain	1956-present
Crescent Toys	Britain	1922-1981
Dinky	Britain	1933-present
Lesney	Britain	1953-present
Spot-On	Britain	1959-1967
Tootsie Toys	USA	1906-present

TOYS 1800-1900

A Günthermann painted tinplate frog, c.1898

Since the earliest known times, children have found toys to play with. Although in early civilisations, such as the Greeks, Romans and Ancient Egyptians, craftsmen are known to have made sophisticated toys for their children out of clay, bone and even bronze, toys were more commonly homemade – carved from wood, sewn from fabric, or simply improvised from everyday objects.

By the 16thC, European children played with toys made from clay and the 17thC saw the introduction of Noah's Arks and rocking horses. By the early 18thC, a blossoming toy industry was established in Germany, providing toys for the children of wealthy parents both in Europe and for the new settlers in America. Nuremberg in southern Germany became the centre of production, making a wide range of toys such as spinning tops and dolls' houses. For the very wealthy, valuable toys, such as miniature porcelain tea sets, were made by factories at Meissen and Chelsea, and silversmiths produced miniature trinkets and sewing kits. The less privileged had more choice too by this time, as shops were set up in many European cities selling toys such as tin solders and rag dolls. Educational toys grew in popularity, including wooden alphabet bricks and puzzles.

Wooden toys continued to be widely produced through-out the 19thC and many pieces are highly collectable today. Favourite subjects for wooden toys include well-established subjects, such as Noah's Arks, rocking horses and wooden figures, as well as large wooden toys, including toboggans and even miniature wheelbarrows.

The earliest surviving pieces, some of which date back to the 17thC are the most sought after, and condition, both of the wood and any paintwork, is crucial to assessing the value of all these toys.

Paper was an important material too, often combined with wood to produce attractive carpet toys in the form of ships or other vehicles and as toy theatres. Juvenile drama became popular from the 18thC onwards, and by the early 19thC publishers and printers were producing sheets of figures and dialogue for children to recreate plays at home. Paper was also used to make attractive and colourful 'scraps' (often in the shape of figures, flowers and animals) which could then be stuck into scrap books. Early pieces were hand-painted, but the introduction of chromolithography from 1860 onwards meant manufacturers could produce large numbers of high-quality printed scraps less expensively.

The 19thC marked a major turning point in the history of toys, with the development of tinplate as the most widely used material, which rapidly dominated the market from the 1850s onwards. When tinplate from South Wales became widely available, large-scale production in factories made it possible to make quite complicated toys inexpensively. The main area of production for tinplate, as with all types of toys, was Germany, with the leading companies including Märklin (established in 1859), Bing (established in 1879) and Carette (established in 1886).

They all produced a wide range of high-quality painted tinplate toys, some afforded only by the very wealthy. Typical subjects included figures and vehicles, such as the horsedrawn carriage and early motor vehicles.

In America, the first tinplate factories were opened in the 1830s, catering for a largely domestic market. The toys were produced for a short period compared with tinplate toys made in Europe, as cast-iron was preferred as a material. Among the most popular toys produced in America were toy banks. These appeared after the American Civil War, when America was swept by a craze for hoarding coins in response to paper money of very low denomination printed by both sides during the war. By the late 1800s, the banks had become quite sophisticated and increasingly popular.

Other cast-iron toys appeared at the same time and many were produced by companies such as the Kenton Hardware Co. From a collector's perspective, the problem with cast-iron is in the nature of the material itself. Although cast-iron is very durable, it is extremely brittle and will break easily if dropped. Therefore, cast-iron toys are often found with damage (almost impossible to repair effectively), and the price of complete pieces will usually reflect their scarcity.

All American toys are scarce in Europe. Tinplate toys, particularly small pull-along animals, are the most easily found, but their condition is often poor.

PAPER & PAPER ON WOOD TOYS (I)

The Neptune Theatre, a toy theatre made by Benjamim Pollock 1880s; 12in (33cm) high; value code G

Note: The range of toys is so vast and varied, that it is not possible to provide a single, definitive checklist.

Juvenile drama

Before the advent of cinema and television, the theatre was the most popular form of inexpensive and enjoyable public entertainment, with dozens of new plays performed in Europe's major cities every year from the 18thC onward.

English toy theatres quickly developed independently from the rest of Europe, and became closely associated with current London stage productions. By the early 19thC, publishers and printers were producing sheets of figures and dialogue for children to recreate plays at home.

The sheets were sold as a 'penny plain or tuppence coloured' and the whole genre

became known as juvenile drama. These theatres were extremely popular with children; as with the real version, characters were always colourful and imaginatively dressed, and theatres often included special effects, such as mechanical wave machines, trap doors and flying phantoms.

Theatre makers

Benjamin Pollock (1856-1937) was one of the best-known publishers of toy theatres. A furrier by trade, he took over his father-in-law's publishing business on his death and proceeded to publish large numbers of play reprints, as well as toy theatres and figures.

Other makers to look out for

include W. Webb (1820-1890), J.K. Green (1790-1860), Hodgson & Co. (1822-1830), John Redington (1819-1876), and George Hieronymous Besteleier (1793-1825).

Publishers and toymakers made a variety of different sized and shaped theatres (to suit the needs of different plays). The toy theatre in the main picture, known as the Neptune theatre, was made by Benjamin Pollock in the late 1880s, and has many features typical of all 19thC toy theatres.
* The proscenium (the arch separating the stage from the auditorium, together with the area immediately in front of the arch) is made of hand-coloured paper on card, backed with strips of wood.
* Makers often used wood from tea chests and other boxes.
* The colourful hand-coloured paper figures are mounted on wood with a long piece of wire attached, so they can be moved off and on stage.
* The characters are performing an elaborate contemporary version of a well-known traditional story (in this case, it is possibly the famous tale of St. George and the Dragon).

This charming early 19thC garden scene (above) reflects the quality of skill involved in making these early paper toys. Made in France c.1830, these hand-coloured and varnished figures are mounted on wooden blocks so they can be moved around the scene. Similar to a toy theatre in concept, this type of toy would have been particularly popular with children who had a fertile imagination.

Scrap

Compiling scrapbooks was a popular pastime for 19thC children and adults. Early scraps were hand-coloured, but from 1860 onwards, with the development of chromolithography, manufacturers produced large numbers of high-quality printed scraps, depicting a wide range of decorative subjects.

* Chromolithography is a printing process by which coloured prints are taken from etched and polished stone, enabling a finer range of tints than is possible from prints using metal plates.

Value

The value of scraps depends on condition, size and subject. Unused sheets, such as this set (above) by an unidentified German maker, reflect the Victorian enthusiasm for nostalgia. Other common subjects include flowers and children, seasonal themes, such as Father Christmas and, most valuable of all, royal figures and processions. Scrapbooks generally tend to be less valuable.

Technique

Inexpensive to produce, cardboard was a popular and versatile material used in a variety of toys, including toy farms. This German farmhouse and figures (below) are part of a set made in 1910, and show how cardboard could successfully be used to produce good-quality toys. Each item has been made from a thick piece of card, giving it solidity, and the detailed chromolithography make them even more appealing.

Collecting

Collectors generally prefer commercially-produced theatres by well-known makers. Home-made versions, although often of a very high standard, are not so popular and are much less valuable. Other paper toys, such as scraps, are sought after too, but are still fairly inexpensive to buy.

PAPER & PAPER ON
WOOD TOYS (II)

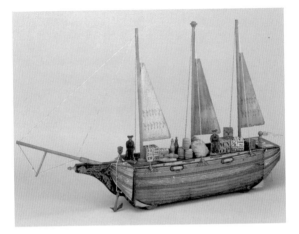

Paper on wood

By combining paper with wood, 19thC toymakers were able to produce a wide range of solidly built toys with attractive and delicate details. Although the materials were less expensive to work with than tinplate, the finished toys were often of an extremely high standard. The wonderful boat in the main picture, the 'Ocean Wave' was made in America by the W.S. Reed Toy Co. in the 1880s and is an excellent example of a good-quality paper and paper on wood toy. The main structure of the ship, including the masts and the rudder, are wooden, while details such as the sails and the sailors

have been made from cardboard, adding variety to the toy's design. The hull of the ship has been covered with chromolithographed paper and several pieces of cargo have been stamped discreetly with the makers' initials.

Forts

Forts were perennially popular toys in the 19thC and early 20thC and this fine paper and wood example (below) would have been made in Germany c.1900. Each part of the fort is detachable and it is in such good condition that it is probable that each piece was carefully put away in the box by the owners every time it was played with.

Technique

Many different techniques and materials were used to produce this unusual magnetic toy town (below), which was made in Germany in the mid-1800s.

For example, the base is wood covered with printed paper, the scenery is made from both printed paper on card (at the back) and printed paper on wood (in the foreground), while the figures are made from composition (a substance made from wood or paper pulp which is mixed with various types of reinforcing ingredients, such as old rags and bits of bone, see also p.10).

As with many paper and wood toys from this period, this toy town would have been fairly inexpensive to produce, even though it has many intricate components and a fairly complicated inner mechanism.

By turning the handle which moves a magnet under the box, the figures are able to move around the town accompanied by a simple musical tune.

Building blocks

One of the earliest types of toys known to exist are building blocks: simple wooden versions are believed to have been used by children in medieval times. By the 19thC, wooden blocks had become more sophisticated, and boxed sets of plain wooden bricks, such as these German architectural bricks from the late 1880s (above), would have been commonly found in most Victorian nurseries.

By the 1860s, wooden blocks were often covered with chromolithographed coloured paper, to form educational toys or six-sided puzzle blocks.

Marks

Paper and paper on wood toys are rarely marked with the makers' name. They were made by numerous different makers across Europe, particularly in German, for export and it is more common to find the label of the shop where the toy was sold.

Condition

Paper is a delicate material and prone to tearing and fading, which can affect the value of a toy greatly.

Nests

Popular with 19thC toddlers, and with young children today, are interlocking nests.
* Often sold in sets of diminishing sizes, such as these three boxes (below), made in Germany c.1910, these colourful cardboard nests were light and easy to store

as they could be contained in a single cube.
* These blocks were made in large numbers and are still fairly easy to find.
* Their value lies in their design – the more detailed and attractive the picture featured, the more desirable they are.

WOODEN TOYS

A wood and composition swing toy, German c.1840; 8in (20.4cm) high; value code C

Identification checklist for wooden toys 1800-1900
1. Is the toy complete?
2. If painted, is the paintwork original and still brightly coloured?
3. Is the wood or paper dirty? (Dirt on wood is difficult to clean off successfully, see below.)
4. Does it have an original box?
5. Is there a pattern number or shop label on the box or on the toy?

Wooden toys
Although wooden toys have been made since Ancient times, the earliest surviving toys mostly date back to the 17thC. These toys are highly sought after today, and command high prices, although they are rarely found in good condition.

Despite the introduction of new materials such as tinplate, wooden toys continued to be widely produced throughout the 19thC and many pieces are highly collectable today. The delightful wooden swing toy in the main picture is typical of many toys with movement produced from the late 18thC in Altdorf near

Nuremberg, where they were known as *leyern*. Toys of a similar style were later produced in the Erzegebirge area of Saxony, also in Germany and these were known as *kumperkisten* and are easily distinguished by their more complicated mechanisms.
* By moving a lever on the side of the toy (not visible here), the couple swing back and forth.
* These toys are extremely rare, owing to their fragility.

American toys
One of the best-known American makers of wooden toys in the mid-19thC was the Crandall family, led by cousins Jesse A. and

Charles M., who produced a wide range of simple constructional wooden toys. In 1867 they patented a unique tongue-and-groove system which allowed the figures to be interlocked in endless permutations.

They went on to apply the principle to wooden figures, such as this toy of John Gilpin and his horse in 1867 (below), based on a character from the 18thC poem, *The Diverting History of John Gilpin* by William Cowper. Some of the Crandall patents were taken up by H. Jewitt & Co. of London, which produced their own version of the jointed figures.

Noah's Arks
These toys have been hugely popular from the 18thC until the present day.

Arks were often just decorated storage boxes for the animals, which were the real focus of interest, although the ark of this set (above), made in Germany c.1850, is very attractive in its own right.
* Many Noah's Ark animals have survived in excellent condition, possibly because the toys were regarded as suitable for Sunday play only, particularly in 19thC Protestant Victorian England.
* Early arks, to the mid-19thC, were mainly made without hulls, but with a gentle curve to the base and are highly collectable.
* Approximate dating is possible by examining details such as the women figures' clothing – high waists are found on earlier examples, reflecting the fashions of the early 19thC.

Ring method
Wooden animals for arks and similar farmyards and zoological gardens were hand-carved using the ring method. A large circle of wood was turned so as to produce the animal in cross section.

The animals were then cut from the ring in slices. The legs were separated and then the details, such as ears and horns, were added.

Technique
Painted wood was often of a very high standard. Each piece of this delicate German wooden egg set (below) made c.1880 has been carefully painted.

* Every piece is covered with a layer of glossy shellac (a varnish).
* The egg cups, butter dish and salt and pepper set were all hand-turned on a lathe.

Condition
Wood can suffer many problems over the years, greatly affecting a toy's desirability. Woodworm makes wood fragile, damp can easily warp or rot the wood or dissolve the glue.
* Original paintwork is highly desirable, so take care when trying to clean a dirty wooden toy. Most paint was either poster or watercolour and so can be easily washed off; therefore, cleaning should be left to professional wood restorers.

LARGE WOODEN TOYS

An English carved and painted wooden rocking horse on sharply bowed rockers mid-19thC; 82in (208cm) long; value code C

Identification checklist for mid-19thC rocking horses
1. Does the rocking horse have bow rockers, rather than a swing stand (see below)?
2. Does it have original dapple grey paintwork?
3. Are the horse's eyes made of glass?
4. Does it have finely modelled neck muscles?
5. Are its mane and tail made of horse hair?
6. Is the horse's head long and narrow and turned to one side?
7. Does the horse still have an original leather harness with brass studs?

Rocking horses
Basic carved wooden horses are among the earliest surviving toys, possibly dating back to early civilisation. By the Middle Ages there are several references to hobby horses in contemporary manuscripts, although rocking horses are not mentioned until the 17thC, when they appear as simple structures with flat board sides instead of legs. By the 19thC rocking horses had become a regular feature in most Victorian nurseries.
*Rocking horses were produced

in a variety of styles. The elegant dapple grey horse in the main picture has many typical features.
* The rockers are quite sharply-bowed, helping to date it accurately to the mid-19thC. As the century progressed, more attention was given to safety and so rockers became shallower, and by the 1870s rockers were often replaced with a swing 'safety' stand, where the horse is hung on metal bars from a secure wooden base.
* The most popular colour for rocking horses is dapple grey.

Note how dark the dapples are on the rocking horse in the main picture – by the end of the century the dapples were fewer and the background was much lighter.

Technique

Rocking horses were generally hand-carved by craftsmen from large blocks of wood. They were produced in large numbers, so each horse is slightly different. Variations were made too – this German rocking horse made c.1910 (below) converts to a pull-along toy when its rockers are removed.

Makers

Many firms produced rocking horses during the 19thC and 20thC. Among the best-known makers to look out for are G.& J. Lines (19th and 20thC), William Gabriel (19thC), Frederick Ayres (1864-1940), Patterson Edwards (19th and 20thC), Baby Carriages Ltd (1884-1958) and Scott & Walker Ltd. (1915-1926).

Other large toys

Large wooden toys offered children a different experience from small, delicate toys; they were sturdy, hard-wearing and demanded greater physical involvement.

This miniature wooden wheelbarrow (above) was made specifically for a wealthy child and even has the original owner's initials painted on it.

Made in England c.1890, it is typical of the type of good-quality outdoor toys that were produced for middle and upper-class children. Similar toys include sets of miniature gardening tools, which are often stencilled with the family's coat-of-arms.

Toboggans were popular outdoor toys too, with the best ones made in America, Canada and Scandinavia, where the weather was particularly favourable for their use. Good quality toboggans, such as this one (below) were produced in America c.1900. It has a steering action and an attractive stencilled design and is extremely desirable. Simpler wooden toboggans are also collectable, although they tend to be less valuable.

* Other collectable large toys in this field include sleighs, carts and wagons, most commonly found in America and Canada.
* It is also possible to find push-along trains, fire engines, gypsy caravans and milk carts.
* G. & J. Lines were the most prolific makers of large wooden toys. Their early mark was a thistle stamped on a metal disc.

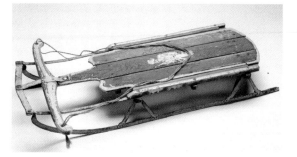

TINPLATE TOYS

A Ludwig Lutz clockwork, hand-painted, tinplate open-deck paddle steamer 'Wilhelm II', 1890; 28in (71cm) long; value code B

Identification checklist for German toy boats 1800-1900
1. Is the boat of solid construction?
2. Does the boat have a distinctive toy-like (rather than a realistic) quality?
3. Are any deck fittings missing?
4. Does the boat loosely represent a period vessel?
5. Is the paintwork original?
6. Are the deck details and paddle boxes oversize for the scale of the model?

European toys
During the first part of the 19thC, Germany's toy industry was the most advanced and dominant in Europe. Although the toys are not as sophisticated in design as they were to become later in the century, following the arrival of makers such as Bing, Märklin and Carette, they are of high quality and extremely desirable.

Lütz (1846-1891)
One of the most important German makers of this era was founded by Ludwig Lütz in Ellwangen. Their factory produced a range of dolls' house furniture, soldiers, carriages and boats, such as the one in the main picture. The quality of these toys was extremely high; at the company's peak, in the 1880s, the company employed over 15 workmen in their factory,

including tinsmiths, welders and tin painters. As can be seen from the intricate and well-crafted detail of the 'Wilhelm II', in the main picture, production must have been costly. Ultimately, the toys were too highly priced for the market, and, in 1891, Lütz sold his stock and equipment to Märklin, founded in 1859. They adapted many of Lütz's designs; however, toys such as this boat, which did not continue to be produced, are more sought after.

Günthermann (1877-1960)
One of the most popular toy-makers of the 19thC was founded by Siegfried Günthermann in 1877, who produced a wide range of tinplate figures and vehicles, all with an individual sense of humour.
* Although machine-pressed, this attractive ragtime dancing couple

excellent condition as they were inadequately primed and the paintwork can flake off extremely easily.

Vehicles

The popularity of clockwork painted tinplate figures in the late 19thC was further increased with the development of toys based on the newly invented horseless carriage. These cars were often far more lively in appearance and design than horse-drawn coaches.

This one (above) appears in the Bing catalogue of 1898 and was possibly made either by Bing or another maker, such as Günthermann, and bought in as stock by Bing.
* It is of particular interest to collectors as it incorporates all the ungainly features of early motor cars. Note the exposed seating, tiller steering, carriage-style wheels and traditional hand-painted tinplate figures.
* Beware of pieces that have been replaced, particularly parts such as headlamps.

(above) are full of movement. Note how expressive their faces are and how the male dancer's coat tails swing as he dances.
* These toys are hard to find in

Rock & Gräner (1815-1905)

Rock & Gräner, another leading toymaker of the 19thC, was founded as early as 1815 and produced a wide range of dolls' house furniture, tinplate trains, signals, lamp-posts, horsedrawn carriages and railway locomotives, as well as a range of hand-painted tinplate dioramas (miniature three-dimensional scenes), such as this example (below right), depicting a large castle in the centre of elaborate scenery.
* Note the water-powered mill, operated by a pump hidden within the castle.
* By 1850 they were the largest toymakers in Germany. By the

1890s, however, the company had gone into decline, were sold in 1896 to Oskar Ebelhaf, another toymaker, and were then known as Rock & Gräner Nachfolger. They continued to produce high quality toys, but closed in 1905.

AMERICAN TOYS
1850-1900

The 'Charles' hose reel by George Brown; c.1867; 23in (58.4cm) long; value code A

Identification checklist for American toys 1850-1900
1. Is the toy made of hand-painted tinplate?
2. Does the toy feature any attractive applied stencil or transfer decoration?
3. Is the condition original?
4. Does it have an elaborate design?
5. Is the maker known?
6. Does the toy have a pull-along mechanism?

American toys
Until the 18thC, the most widely available toys in America were those produced at home by settlers for their children. Carved from wood into simple figures, dolls and animals, these toys are now highly sought after by collectors. Other, more sophisticated, wooden toys, such as hoops, rocking horses and tops were imported from Europe, but could be afforded only by the very wealthy.

By the 19thC an indigenous toy industry had developed in America, and a wealth of craftsmen were able to produce a wider selection of wooden toys. Among the most famous companies were William S. Tower of South Hingham, Massachusetts, who founded the Tower Toy Company in 1830, producing wooden toys, dolls and dolls' houses, and the Crandall family, who produced toys such as rocking horses, building blocks and figures (see pp. 20 and 24).

Tinplate
The best-known tinplate toymakers in the mid-19thC was George Brown & Co., which made the magnificent 'Charles' hose reel in the main picture. Born in 1830, Brown started his toy business in 1856 after training as a clockmaker, and he became the first person to incorporate a mechanism into American toys.

George Brown's toys represented a cross-section of America life from a pioneering period in American history.

Although the 'Charles' is an extremely rare and valuable toy (it currently holds the world-record price for any toy sold at auction), it has many typical features to look out for in all American 19thC tinplate toys:
* made of tinplate and hand-painted
* ingenious design
* careful decoration
* lightness of touch
* pull-along mechanism.

In contrast to the modern 'Charles', is this horse-drawn gig c.1870 (right) – a wonderful evocation of a Southern gentleman-farmer out for a trot.
* It features the newly introduced clockwork mechanism and the wheel-driven trotting action of the horses (popular in America).

J. & E. Stevens (1843-c.1930)

In 1868, the toymaker, George Brown, merged with J. & E. Stevens, a company founded in 1843 by John and Elisha Stevens, who were makers of cast iron hardware. By the 1850s, the two Stevens brothers produced toys in their own right, as well as providing various components for other toymakers.
* If a toys is marked, it will often include the date the toy was patented. This velocipede (below) is marked 'Stevens & Brown, patented Jan 25 and Feb 1st 1870'.

This comic cast-iron monkey cyclist on a pull-along tricycle was made by J. & E. Stevens (see above) c.1890.
* It is solidly constructed.
* At this time, cast-iron toys were generally in the form of static playthings, such as banks (see p.30), making this pull-along comic monkey very unusual.
* Cast-iron vehicles became popular later, after 1900.
* This piece incorporates a ringing bell (a popular feature in American toys), introduced in the late 1860s by the Gong Bell Co.

* Toys are often made from several different materials and are very fragile. This one has a stiffened cloth-headed doll driver, with coloured fabric clothes and brass hands and legs.

Cast-iron

Cast-iron toys were first produced in the late 1860s, although, other than banks, they were not made in great numbers until the 1880s.
* To make cast-iron toys, wooden patterns of the component required were packed in special casting sand, with blow holes. The sand box was then split, the wooden patterns removed, the box reassembled and molten iron poured in.
* Once cooled, the casting sand was cleaned off, the sprues removed and the castings fettled to remove any rough edges.

Repair and restoration

Repair to a cast-iron toy or bank is acceptable to collectors, provided it is competently carried out. Repainting is not so desirable, although if it has been well done it can be difficult to detect without the aid of an ultra-violet light. Seek advice before attempting to restore or repaint an old toy.

Collecting

American toys are scarce in Europe. Cast-iron toys are often reproduced (see pp.30-31), so buy with care. Tinplate toys, particularly small pull-along animals, are more easily found, but, although the paintwork is of high quality, usually the priming is not, and the paint tends to flake.

U.S. MECHANICAL &
STILL BANKS 1869-1900

The 'Two Frogs', a hand-painted cast-iron bank, designed by James H. Bowen for J & E Stevens; c.1882; 8½in (21.6cm) long; value code D

Identification checklist for American mechanical banks 1869-1910
1. Is the toy made of cast iron?
2. Is the paintwork in almost perfect condition?
3. Does the bank have a mechanism?
4. Does the mechanism work?
5. Is the coin trap present (see below)?
6. Can you see a patent mark underneath the toy?

Banks
Although mechanical and 'still' (without a mechanism), money banks had existed for centuries in various materials, such as metal, wood and ceramic, and are still made today, their heyday was in America between 1869 and 1910, when most of the finest designs were made from cast iron.

Following the American Civil War, between 1861 and 1865, there was a shortage of coinage and an understandable desire for thrift. As a result, money banks became a popular way in which to encourage children to save money.

As well as having this serious side, banks were often humorous, such as the 'Two Frogs' mechanical bank in the main picture, which depicts two life-like frogs seated in pond weed.
* The mechanism involves the smaller frog kicking a coin into the larger frog's mouth when a lever (hidden in the picture) is pressed.

Kyser & Rex (1879-1898)
Another famous manufacturer was Kyser & Rex, which made this 'Monkey and Lion' bank.
* This popular bank exemplifies the ingenious devices employed: the larger monkey casts a coin into the hungry lion's mouth, while the baby monkey jumps on to his mother's shoulders.
* Other important banks include

the 'Hall's Excelsior', which was patented in 1869 by John Hall and produced by J. & E. Stevens (the first major iron toy company, eventually known as the American Toy Company). Designed to represent the equivocal relationship between bank and customer, it features a bank cashier in the form of a monkey, which snatches the coins and pops them in the bank.

Shephard Hardware Co. (1882-1892)

One of their most important banks was this 'Trick Dog' bank (below), where, when the coin is placed in the dog's mouth and the lever is pressed, the dog jumps through the hoop and deposits the coin in the barrel.
* Other banks produced by Shephard include Punch and Judy and Uncle Sam.
* Although most banks, such as this one, were made in cast-iron, look for types made in lead, wood and tinplate too. They are often less valuable, but still attractive.

Post-1900

Although bank production continued until the 1940s, it was on a much smaller scale. The main reason for their decline was the rise in material costs after the two World Wars, when iron ore was in demand to make weapons.

English variants

Although America was the home of the cast-iron bank, other countries, such as Britain, produced them too, from the 19thC well into the 1930s.

This 'Speaking Dog Bank' (above right) was made by John Harper & Co. Ltd, c.1902, and is almost identical to a bank made by Shephard Hardware Co.

It is easy to distinguish, as the Harper version does not carry the Shephard patent mark, but is worth about the same.

Still banks

To complement mechanical banks, manufacturers produced a range of still banks. These banks had no mechanisms and were generally plainer in design, but can still be collectable.

Condition

As an almost exclusively American product, rare examples are at a premium. Condition is crucial to value too – this 'Donkey Bank' (below), by J. & E. Stevens c.1880s, is in excellent condition and is complete with its wooden packing case.
* As such, it is worth ten times as much as an identical one in only reasonable condition.

Reproductions

Because of the simplicity of the casting process, there are now far more reproductions on the market than originals, and these are of little value. Points to look out for on reproductions include:
* badly-finished castings, particularly where sections join
* poorly-modelled base, with a blank panel where 'Taiwan' was taken out of the mould,
* artificially aged in wet sand,
* modern internal components in the mechanism.

A Carette tinplate carpet toy sailing boat, c.1905

By the turn of the 19thC, Germany had a well-established lead in the field of toy manufacture, and toys made by famous firms, such as Märklin, Bing and Carette, were considered to be the best of their kind in the world. Toy shops flourished too, with stores such as Gamages and Harrods in London and Le Nain Bleu in Paris, offering an enormous range of European-made toys.

The Edwardian period was also a time of comparative peace and affluence in many European countries, enabling the toy industry to maintain a high standard of production. Contemporary events and developments were important factors in the choice of design and subject matter of these new toys. Tinplate was still the most widely-used material and was designed to represent a wealth of subjects. Horse-drawn carriages, boats, submarines, aeroplanes and even airships were made, reflecting contemporary changes in actual transport during this era.

One of the most influential events on toymaking at this time was the invention of the motor car. Models of its predecessors, horse-drawn carriages and carts, had been very popular in the 19thC, but the motor car offered far more scope and variety to toy designers and more fun for children. By 1900, makers were fully aware of the sales value of toy cars and so coupés, tourers, racing cars and the fashionable double phaetons were quickly put into production. The resulting toys were of a very high standard, and the best ones, by makers such as Märklin and Bing, also included well-finished interiors and details such as miniature lamps, travelling rugs and luggage.

Toy cars, in common with most tinplate toys of this era,

were usually hand-painted, expecially those made by top companies, such as Bing and Märklin. The paintwork was usually of a very high quality too, and many examples have survived in good condition today, although over-zealous restoration is often a danger.

Other popular subjects for toys included fairgrounds amusements and circuses, as well as novelty figures. One of the greatest exponents in this field was Ernst Lehmann. A German toymaker, Lehmann designed an exceptionally fine range of lithographed and painted tinplate figures, all executed with a strong sense of humour. Other companies imitated his designs, but they are generally easy to spot, as they are of much poorer quality.

With retail demand for high-quality toys satisfied by Germany, there was little demand for domestically produced tinplate toys in other European countries. In France, the major toy producer was Fernand Martin, who made high-quality and attractive novelty figures, while in Britain, in 1901, the toymaker, Frank Hornby, created 'Mechanics Made Easy'. These were constructional sets that could be used to build a variety of buildings and objects. The idea came to him from watching a crane at work, when it occurred to him that models could easily be made out of a small number of simple parts.

In 1907, he changed the name to Meccano. Hornby were to become one of the most important British toymakers of this century, particularly during the inter-war years, when they introduced the Hornby Series of toy railways and the highly successful Dinky Toy range.

The other significant development in the toy industry in Britain at this time was the rise of the biscuit tin industry. Biscuit tins were designed by makers such as Barringer Wallis & Manners and Huntley, Boorne & Stevens for biscuit makers and were an imaginative marketing tool. The tins came in a range of attractive novelty and toylike shapes, most popularly in the form of transport vehicles such as vans. These would often have a panel on the side advertising the biscuit makers' name. Unlike some toys, these tins were lithographed rather than hand-painted, making them relatively affordable for all markets.

Other popular and inexpensive toys in Europe during this period were penny toys. True to their name, they were keenly-priced toys, made from colourful lithographed tinplate with a simple, push-along action. Germany was the main producer and these toys were sold throughout Europe by street vendors. They quickly achieved a widespread popularity, peaking in production in 1906.

In America, the toy market continued to develop independently from Europe. Mechanical banks were still produced, as well as a range of horse-drawn and motorized vehicles.

Toys from this period are highly collectable today, with enormous prices paid for top-quality products. However, at the lower end of the range it is still possible to find less expensive but attractive items too.

BING CARS 1900-1914

A Bing Brake motor car; c.1900; 7in (17.6cm) long, value code B

Identification checklist for Bing cars 1900-1914
1 Does the car have a maker's mark?
2. Are there any distinctive features to identify the maker (see below)?
3. Is the paintwork original?
4. Is the car complete with all its original parts, including the clockwork mechanism (if not, this will lower value)?
5. Is the design shown in contemporary catalogues?
6. Are the wheels plain-spoked?
7. Does the design emulate features on contemporary motor cars?

Bing (c.1879-1933)
After Märklin, (see p.36) the leading German manufacturers of quality tinplate toys were Gebrüder Bing, who specialized in boats, cars and trains. The brothers Ignatz and Adolf Bing established a strong reputation for producing fine quality, expensive toys, often sold in specially designed presentation boxes. As with other famous German toy firms of this period, their output of the most expensive toys was fairly small until 1914 and so toys which have survived are highly sought after by collectors.

Distinctive features
Bing designed their toy cars with far more mechanical accuracy than competitors such as Märklin (although only loosely based on actual models), but with realistic details, such as glass windows and door handles. One of the earliest known models of an actual motor car, the Bing Brake in the main picture, has an ingenious random steering action.

Main characteristics of pre-1914 Bing cars:
* the De Dion Bouton-style coal scuttle bonnet (seen in pre-1904 toys), which was named after the shape of bonnet used on actual contemporary De Dion Bouton motor cars:
* the attention to realistic detail – designs were often based on contemporary cars
* the light construction
* the fine quality hand-painted and lined finish
* powerful springs which allowed the cars to run for long periods
* a uniformed chauffeur often included in the car.

Although this 'American Platform' motor fire truck, c.1904 (above) has similar lamps to the Bing Brake, its steering action is very different – simpler and with a spring-loaded ratchet visible at the top of the steering column, which fixes the wheels in a particular direction. Loosely based on a real model, this design illustrates Bing's expertise in combining originality with mechanical precision. It is interesting to note how it is made up of components from a variety of different models – the platforms are raised by a rack and pinion turned by a ship's wheel and the firemen would be protected by the same type of posts and handrails as used in Bing's toy boats. Its most novel feature though, mentioned in contemporary Bing catalogues, is its 'Tuff-Tuff' leather bellows, which reproduced the wheezing sound of early motor engines. (To have original parts still in working order is very desirable.)

Bing often made the same models in different colours. This four-seat open tourer (above), c.1912, shows advances made both in real and toy car design. A far cheaper model than the Bing limousine from 1908 (below), it is made of lithographed tinplate with simply pressed wheels, wings and seats and the squared-off shape of the 1908 bonnet has been replaced by a more modern convex one. This version was produced in much larger quantities than earlier cars. They are therefore much less valuable, particularly if they have suffered damage.

Wheels

Early models, such as the Bing Brake, generally have plain wheels, like carriage wheels, with thin, spindly spokes and rims. Later, less expensive models had plain, thick spokes, and, by 1914, they tended to be finely-detailed, cast 'artillery' wheels. These were spoked wheels with a tyre of stretched rubber.

This Bing four-seat open tourer (above), introduced in 1904, is in a more modern style than the Bing Brake. Elegantly designed from a contemporary Double Phaeton, its seats may look comfortable enough to sit on, but in fact they are made of cast lead! The mud guards are missing on this example, but its artillery wheels (see below) are clearly visible as is the rakish bonnet with separate brass louvre pressings.
* The tourer was produced in three sizes from 10in (25cm) to 14in (35 cm) long; this is the largest version.

Packaging
Original packaging is extremely rare, as boxes were often thrown away soon after purchase, and they can add substantially to the value. The unusual survival of the original box for an early Bing limousine (above), c.1908, is particularly interesting to collectors; the box still carries the label showing the early Bing trademark and a carefully written pencil inscription: 'automobile'.

Collecting
Size and value vary greatly; large cars tend to have more details and so command the highest prices. Original paintwork is particularly important, so do not be tempted to repaint damaged parts.

MÄRKLIN & OTHER
GERMAN CARS 1900-1914

*A Märklin limousine c.1910; 12in (4.8cm) long;
value code B.*

Identification checklist for Märklin cars
1. Is the car solid and well-built?
2. Is the paintwork thickly, but finely applied and original?
3. Does the car have a complex steering mechanism?
4. Are all the parts original?
6. Does the luggage rack have a pierced design?
7. Does the car have a plain, but sturdy appearance?
8. Does it represent a contemporary vehicle?

Märklin (1859-present)
Märklin produced high quality, expensive toys in small numbers with a limited range and continue to do so today. Prices are generally high for all Märklin cars and among the rarest models are specially commissioned lorries and buses. The value of the 1910 limousine in the main picture is lowered as there has been some restoration and the lamps have been replaced.

Made from heavy gauge tin-plate with decorative paintwork, it is typical of Märklin cars of this period. Other distinctive features include:
* realistic details (luggage straps and removable spare tyres)
* unusual lamps with concave lenses (replacement lamps will appear too shiny)
* 'waisted' wheel spokes (difficult to reproduce)
* a unique worm-drive steering action, operating on an open rack.

Carette (1886-1917)
Carette were one of the most prolific toy car manufacturers of this era. Although based in Nuremberg, Georges Carette was originally from France, where he was forced to return at the start of World War I.

Early Carette models from c.1904 are generally made of gaudily lithographed lightweight tinplate. They sometimes feature a distinct gold lining along the paintwork, which can be seen in this two attractive seat open touring car (below).

The touring car has many features typical of many Carette motor cars made during the pre-World War I period:
* concave brackets connecting the running boards to the subframe
* simply pressed one-piece wheels
* painted chauffeur
* coal-scuttle-shape bonnet.

The most famous and desirable of all Carette's toys is this four-light (i.e. four-side windows) limousine, made c.1911 (below).

Built in three different sizes 8½in (22cm), 12½in (32cm) and 16in (40cm) long and in different versions, the cars originally cost between 1s 9d and 20 shillings. This version is in the middle price range and size and includes extras, such as glass windows and a chauffeur. However, it is the largest and most expensive cars, produced in fewer numbers and with finer details, which are the most desirable. Hand-painted, these versions were delicately lined and fitted with a neat wire roof rack with cast brackets. White rubber tyres and artillery wheels were used on the top models too, while others had tyres and wheels made from a one-piece metal pressing.

Günthermann (1877-1960)
Whereas Märklin cars may sometimes seem rather staid and solid, Günthermann cars have a sense of fun, as in this four-seat open tourer (below), with beautifully hand-painted tinplate figures.

Figures
The Günthermann factory specialized in producing a range of novelty child and adult figures in everyday poses, such as flying a kite, dancing or even mopping the floor, all with a light-hearted sense of humour lacking in many Edwardian toys (see p.16). The well-dressed but upright figures in this car definitely seem to be on an outing in their Sunday best! (A car with figures missing loses half its value.)

Marks
Only the most expensive models are marked.

Condition
Günthermann was a prolific manufacturer by contemporary standards. Many cars have survived, so good condition is particularly important. Unfortunately, these toys are prone to damage as they are relatively flimsy, so handle them with care.

Hess (1826-1934)
Johann Hess produced an innovative fly-wheel driven mechanism (in place of the usual clockwork system), which was used in a range of open and closed tourers.
   This 1905 racer (below) is particularly impressive. Its long bonnet encloses the fly-wheel mechanism and is driven by a crank handle. It is worth more than twice as much as the tourer equivalent. Remarkably, the mechanisms are often still in working order.

Value
Perhaps because many cars have survived to the present day and because the colouring is more subdued than in other lithographed vehicles, Hess cars are less expensive to purchase than those manufactured by some other toymakers.
   When small parts, such as the steering wheel, are missing the value is actually reduced only slightly, but more serious damage can reduce the value.

MÄRKLIN BOATS

*A Märklin painted tinplate clockwork steamboat, the 'Shamrock II';
c.1909; 20in (50cm) long; value code B*

Identification checklist for Märklin boats 1900-1914
**1. Is the paintwork original? (Boats are often repainted
as they tend to suffer greatly from damage.)**
**2. Is the boat generally free from rust ? (This affects
price greatly.)**
**3. Does it have the original mechanism (either
clockwork, steam or electric)?**
4. Are the portholes hand-painted?
**5. Are all the deck fittings, lifeboats, masts and
pennants present?**
6. Is there a maker's mark?

Märklin boats
Märklin boats were solidly built,
with a fine quality hand-painted
hull and deck detailing. Size and
shape varied considerably, from
the colourful exuberance of the
'Shamrock II' (above) to the
majestic 'Augusta Victoria', which
was a little under 4ft long!
Smaller, less expensive liners,
steamboats and battleships were
made in greater numbers and the
'Jolanda' (above right) remained
in production until well after
World War I.

Main Features
The 'Shamrock II' riverboat is
immediately recognizable as a
Märklin boat from this period.
Look for the typical features:

* distinctive solid appearance
* thick lining around the portholes and on the deck planking
* a heavy paint finish to even the
smallest component (referred
to as 'hand-enamelled' by
Märklin in their toy catalogues of
this period)
* Märklin trademark on rudder
* wave-painted base
* decoratively-pierced windows.
  The excellent condition in
which this vessel has remained
can be partly explained by its history: its original owners, who had
kept her for over 80 years, were
given her as children and were
never allowed to go sailing without each of them holding a separate line from the boat to the
shore to ensure its safe return.

Clockwork

Most boats were powered by a strong clockwork motor with the key arbour located in one of the stacks (funnels), such as the 'Shamrock II', as well as the 'Jolanda' (below).

This attractive steam yacht from c.1909, was one of the most popular and long-running model boats ever produced by Märklin. Powered by a clockwork mechanism, it combines a sturdy hull with planked effect on the deck and is an excellent representation of a real yacht used in Germany's African colonies.

Ocean Liners

Märklin boats were powered by clockwork, steam or electricity, in order of expense. The fine 38in (98cm) liner 'Lepanto' (below) has a horizontal boiler with two linked vertical engines driving twin screws; although in good condition, she clearly has had some use, as the stern is ½in (1cm) shorter than when new, proving the power of her mighty engines when in contact with the edge of a pond! Most sought after and expensive of all is the 'Augusta Victoria'. At 118cm in length – nearly 4ft – she looks almost identical to the 'Lepanto', or the 'Mauretania' for the British

market, but her massive hull houses batteries with enough power to run for several hours.

Usually built between 1909 and 1912, although available after World War I, these fine liners represent the pinnacle of toy boat manufacture. Märklin were the only makers to produce vessels of this calibre and expense – they were largely built to special order and a batch could take up to six months to complete. Sadly, only a few examples have survived, making them extremely valuable.

Steam

After 20 years of toy warship production during peacetime, warships such as the steam-powered 'Nürnberg' are particularly interesting as it was produced during World War I. This example (below) appears in Märklin's wartime catalogue.

As with Bing, this catalogue concentrated on special wartime models. The 'Nürnberg' used a spirit-fired boiler, in common with all steam engine-powered boats. Steam-powered boats were extremely prone to damage because of the heat generated. Although there is some scorching clearly visible below the deck line, this boat has survived remarkably well.

BING & OTHER
GERMAN BOATS

A Bing clockwork painted tinplate American-outline twin-stack steamer, the 'Columbia'; 1906; 25in (65cm) long; value code C.

Identification checklist for Bing boats 1890-1914

1. Does the boat have typical Bing portholes (see below)?
2. Is the boat's paintwork original?
3. Does the boat have a plain tan-coloured deck, embossed with a trademark plate or transfer?
4. Does it have a mechanism, either clockwork, live steam or electric?
5. Are the deck fittings original and undamaged?
6. Is the hull a distinctive shape (see below)?

Bing boats

As part of the contemporary fascination with the latest modes of transport, Bing, the world's largest toymakers during this period, produced a wide range of toy boats to suit all pockets, and to rival competing Märklin products (see p.38).

This elegant steamer, the 'Columbia' in the main picture, was made at the height of their production, and has many characteristics typical of all Bing boats:
* lightness of touch, compared with the thickly painted and sturdy style of Märklin
* transfer portholes (rather than painted or stamped on)
* attention to realistic details – designs often closely based on real vessels
* a distinctive, streamlined shape.

Dating Bing boats

Bing produced two series of boats in the period leading up to World War I, the most valuable of which is the First Series.

First Series (1890-1910)
* Boats from this series, such as the 'Columbia', are rare and are often heavily restored.
* They range in size from 25-29 ½in (64-75cm) long.
* They have up to three masts, two propellers, two stacks (funnels) and six lifeboats.
* Most boats, including the 'Columbia', are propelled by a clockwork motor.
* The boats have elegant bow decoration – still in good condition on the 'Columbia'.
* The gunwale (the upper part of the bow) is not as high as the double height on Second Series boats. (Vessels such as the 'Columbia' steamer had no gunwale at all.)

Second Series (1910-1914)
* Boats still had a high-quality finish, but with simpler designs.
* They range in size from 7-37in (18-94cm) long.
* They often have electrically powered motors.

* The overall shape of the whole pressing remained virtually identical, but the superstructure was different, the portholes were updated and the general appearance was more modern.

Variety of Bing boats

Liners were only a small part of their production, which ranged from an economic range of plain, lozenger-shaped submarines to river steamers, battleships and torpedo boats. The development of naval vessels reflected the growing strength of Germany's real naval force, and culminated in the wartime catalogue of 1915, which featured vessels and vehicles used in the current war.

Although this large battle ship (above), from c.1909 (end of First Series), has been poorly restored and has parts missing, it demonstrates the impressive scale of Bing's toy warships. It still shows the cast bow decoration typical of Bing and the Dreadnought prow, but is much plainer overall than the finely detailed warships that were produced c.1900.

Other boat makers

Other major German makers include Carette, Schönner, Hess, Plank, Falk, Arnold and Fleischmann.

Fleischmann (1887-present)

This firm produced only a few fine liners before 1914, all of which were based on the real German Norddeutscher-Lloyd ships, such as the 'Krönprinzess Cecilie' (below) from 1910.

However, it is thought that they made the hull pressings for several other important makers, and they continued making good-quality and popular boats and ships up until the 1950s in a wide range of sizes and prices.

Carette (1886-1917)

This typical Carette boat (below), made c.1905, is a simple but attractively detailed cargo vessel powered by steam, as can be seen from the scorching to the centre section and funnel. Although the paintwork is original, it has restored masts and pennants, which reduces its value slightly.

Carette boats tend to be much simpler than those of Bing or

Märklin. They are often distinguished by a plain hull with horizontal ribs near the deck, which can be seen in this example.

Schönner (1875-1910)

Schönner specialized in small, decorative river boats, although they are also known for their rarer large torpedo boats and the battleship, the 'Aviso Greif' (below), made in 1900.

This small river boat has a typical simple hull, a painted awning, an open horizontal boiler

and a small passenger cabin (the funnel is a replacements) .

Unable to compete with the larger companies, the firm closed in 1910, so their toys are particularly sought after.

Collecting

It is cheaper to start collecting small boats, but always wise to buy the best examples possible.

OTHER TINPLATE TOYS (I)

A Märklin gyroscopic 'Circus Centricus' with figures; c.1909; 20in (52cm) square; ; value code A

Note: The range of toys is so vast and varied, that it is not possible to provide a single, definitive checklist.

Germany

The great German toymakers did not content themselves just with representations of modern transport, but produced a wide range of inventive and high-quality novelty toys.

Using components and pressings from other models, Märklin and Bing were able to produce a wide range of toys. The elaborate 'Circus Centricus' in the main picture, made by Märklin, came with every available piece listed separately, so the child could make up a circus ring.

* Circuses and fairground toys were made by other makers too, such as this carousel (right) by Müller & Kaededer c.1910.

Stock
Wilhelm Stock made this polar sledge (right), reflecting the Edwardian interest in polar exploration. Their toys are more affordable than those by better-known German toymakers.

Ernst Plank (1866-c.1935)
The superb quality of German toys was not confined to just the most famous manufacturers. Ernst Plank of Nuremberg produced some of the most inventive ranges of novelty toys of this period, creating miniature tinplate cars and boats, as well as an extensive range of magic lanterns and experimental toys.
* Optical toys are a fascinating field to collect and they can still be readily found in good condition, complete with fitted boxes and chromolithographic slides, for very reasonable prices.

Aircraft
Not surprisingly, toy aircraft competed closely with cars in popularity with Edwardian children. France was one of the main centres for toy aeroplanes, while Germany produced a wide range of Zeppelin airships.
* The best were modelled in heavy, hand-painted tinplate, but they were also made in lightweight lithographed tinplate. Makers of aircraft included Günthermann, while Lehmann produced a card and tinplate model of similar form, which was known as 'Ikarus'.

France
France's greatest tinplate toy maker was Fernand Martin (1849-1919), who created a comic and inventive range of clockwork, painted tinplate and fabric toys.
* Rather surprisingly, these toys were sold by street vendors and not in shops, a fact which belies their quality and appeal. Today they are very valuable.

Collecting
Martin's toys are highly valued, but watch out for copies. Other European toymakers, such as Ernst Lehmann, made similar versions during this period. Less expensive makers include Wilhelm Stock.

Lehmann
Given the considerable quality of Lehmann toys and the attention to technical details, it is remarkable that they were retailed through local street vendors, in the same way as penny toys (see p.44) and toys by the French toymaker, Fernand Martin (above). It has even been said that a street vendor used to demonstrate Lehmann toys in front of Cologne Cathedral in Germany!

Inspired by the inventive mind of the founder, Ernst Lehmann, the company's toys cover a diverse range of subjects from human figures to animals, all of which were executed with a strong sense of humour.

One of the most popular Lehmann toys ever produced is the amusing 'Mandarin Sedan' chair (left) – note how the mandarin is cheerfully tugging the pigtails of the unfortunate coolie!

Lehmann is also known to have modelled toy figures on his friends and even his family. Typical features found on all Lehmann's toys include:
* finely lithographed and painted tinplate
* spring motors
* rare to see examples in the original box.

Lehmann's toys were widely copied by makers all across Europe, but these are generally of poorer quality and are less sought after by collectors.

OTHER TINPLATE
TOYS (II)

America

The American market continued to be independent of Europe and to develop separately. Mechanical banks were still being produced, as well as a wide range of horse-drawn and early motorized vehicles by Hubley, Dent, Arcade and Kenton. These are now highly collectable in America, but have to be in perfect condition to be of optimum value.

Several new companies came to prominence in America too at this time. In 1913, A.C. Gilbert introduced the 'Erector' toy set to rival Meccano, while Strauss & Co. started a tinplate toy company. The most famous though, was Samuel Dowst, a publisher, who saw a Linotype machine for diecasting printers' type at the Chicago Columbian Exposition of 1893. He adapted it for his own purposes, and, in 1911, produced his first diecast car with turning wheels.

He named the company 'Tootsie Toys' in 1922, inspiring Frank Hornby to create the Dinky Toy range in 1934.

Other popular toys to look out for include a variety of syndicated characters from early cartoon strips such as 'The Yellow Kid', 'Buster Brown and Tige', 'Little Nemo' 'Foxy Grandpa' and the 'Katzenjammer Kids', seen in the main picture in a cast-iron donkey cart.

Another uniquely American toy was this 'Hill Climber' (right) from a series by Clark & Co. of Dayton, Ohio, made of colourful painted pressed steel.

To enable it to go up 'hills', it has a large iron flywheel which drives an extra set of wheels, although it actually barely moves on a flat surface.

* This example probably represents the American entry to the 1903 Gordon-Bennett Racing Trophy in Ireland, as it is finished in the red colours of the American team.
* As with most American toys, apart from mechanical banks (see pp.30-31), they are rarely found in Britain.

Penny Toys

True to their name, penny toys were inexpensive toys, made from colourful lithographed tinplate with a simple push-along action.

Germany was the main producer of penny toys, exporting them to all parts of Europe.
* Some of the main makers to look out for in this field, each with their own miniature logo or recognizable features include Meier, Fischer, Hess and Distler.

First produced in the early 1900s for the pocket money market, they were sold in towns throughout Europe by street vendors. They quickly achieved widespread popularity, peaking in production in 1906, but available up until the 1930s in plainer forms. Their sudden rise to popularity was even commemorated in contemporary popular songs!

Penny toys came in a variety of shapes and styles, such as the military boat wagon for pontoon bridges (above), horse ambulance vehicles, including the very rare 'Dumb Friend's League' ambulance for rescuing horses from the streets of London, early motor cars, aircraft, boats and novelty items. Among some of the even rarer pieces are early telephones, bird cages and even miniature sewing machines.
* Penny toys generally measured between 2-4in (8-10cm) in length. Vehicles were sometimes powered by a fly-wheel drive.
* As many penny toys were produced over a long period, they have to be dated by their colour and the general quality of their construction.

The general rule is that the earlier they were made, the finer the quality.

Collecting
Simple examples of later models from the 1920s are less valuable than rare early horse-drawn or novelty toys. Relatively few are marked, as they were made by many small firms which sold their products through large wholesalers, such as Moses Kohnstam, who traded as Moko.

Britain
With retail demand for high quality toys satisfied by Germany, there was little demand for domestically produced tinplate toys, apart from Frank Hornby's highly successful Meccano system (see p.68).

An exception to this was the development of the British toy biscuit tin industry in the early 20thC. Biscuit tins were designed in a range of attractive novelty and toy-like shapes by specialised tinprinters, including:
* Barringer Wallis & Manners
* Huntley, Boorne & Stevens.

These firms made tins for biscuit makers such as Crawfords, Huntley & Palmer, Peek Frean and Gray Dunn.

This biscuit tin (above), in the form of a finely lithographed tinplate delivery van, was made by Huntley, Boorne & Stevens for the biscuit makers, Macfarlane Lang in 1912. It has many characteristics typical of the best British biscuit tins:
* Transport theme popular, with buses, delivery vans and locomotives produced in large numbers, and, later, aircraft and racing cars.
* An imaginative design. The drivers are printed on flat tinplate, but there is so much detail – even shadows – that they almost appear three-dimensional.
* Interestingly, a much more colourful version of the tin from the same pressing was made for Peek Frean.
* The roof of the van is the hinged lid of the tin.

Condition
The lithography on these tins is extremely thin and prone to rusting and fading; any damage will greatly affect value. The earlier ones are the most sought after.

*A Märklin Gauge I 'Central' railway station and two clerestory
Märklin coaches, c.1910*

Toy trains made in Europe at the turn of the century were
often imaginatively designed but simply made. They under-
went a major development in the early years of the 20thC
after Märklin introduced a regular system of gauges and
they were quick to update and improve their range of trains
during the early part of the 20thC, accompanying them
with an ever larger range of rolling stock, stations, figures
and accessories.

Elsewhere, lightweight, tinplate French carpet toy trains
by makers such as Dessin and Favre, were delicately
detailed, but they were no more advanced than the brass
'dribblers' and 'piddlers' made in Britain (see p.56). In
Germany, trains produced by Rock and Gräner and Ernst
Plank fell into the same category.

Mechanism was an important factor in toy train manufacture and in this period it was provided by steam, clockwork
or highly dangerous early electric motors. Märklin introduced electric motors in 1898, and by 1900 had several different alternating current designs, including four-volt, eight-
volt and the potentially dangerous 110-250 volt.

These different voltages were necessary to cope with the
varied system of AC/DC current available at a time when
there was no unitary electricity system. Other makers introduced these mechanisms too, although less expensive
ranges were powered by clockwork. Carpet toy trains were
also made, which were simply pulled along by the child by
a piece of string.

This was a highly productive time for Germany, with
ready markets for their products throughout Europe. One of
their most important customers was Britain. At the height of
its imperial power and wealth, many families could still

afford high-quality and expensive products. Bing, Märklin's main rival, were also extremely successful in exploiting this market. An important development for Bing occurred when Stefan Bing, son of the founder, met the British entrepreneur, Wenman Bassett-Lowke, at the 1900 Paris Toy Exhibition. At the time, Bassett-Lowke was a model component supplier and he made an agreement with Bing, which was to mark the start of a highly successful and profitable relationship between the two companies.

This working relationship combined the manufacturing skills of Bing with Bassett-Lowke's marketing skill and the creative ability of designer Henry Greenly. Bing made a wide range of trains for Bassett-Lowke which sold them to the British market, initially through a lavish mail-order catalogue and later through an equally successful shop on High Holborn in London.

Bassett-Lowke offered children a complete world of trains, with locomotives, rolling stock and a comprehensive range of accessories, such as tinplate signal boxes and station figures. However, Bassett-Lowke did not rely solely on Bing; Carette also manufactured much material for Bassett-Lowke towards the end of this period.

The introduction of offset lithography, with the invention of printing by drum rather than flat plates in 1903, had a major impact on toymaking of all sorts during this period. It meant that the technique of using lightweight tabbed lithographed tinplate was able to augment painted tinplate in toymaking. It was known as the 'Nuremberg style' after the toymaking centre where it was introduced, particularly by firms such as Bing. In spite of many successes, several of the leading German toymakers closed down during this era, such as Schönner, and Rock & Gräner, with Carette following them in 1917.

Many trains made at this time were in large gauges, most commonly Gauge II, III and IV, which took up a large amount of space to set up. Usually of the highest quality, they are full of appealing details, such as coach interiors crammed with period detail and composition station figures. Postal cars often contain desks and ledgers, while toy dining cars have well-equipped kitchens and the rare Märklin Prison Wagon even has a row of forbidding cells.

America had its own successful toy train industry. Makers such as Lionel and Ives produced a range of popular trains in the large 'Standard' Gauge.

From a collector's perspective, this is not an area to dip into unawares. It is not a large market and is based on very specialised and very knowledgeable collectors and enthusiasts. These collectors have high standards and so condition is extremely important.

The charm of early pieces lies in the delicate hand-enamelling and lining, so scorching, accidental damage or clumsy repainting can make a huge difference to value. Check mechanisms have not been replaced and that all the springs are intact; all these factors will affect value.

MÄRKLIN TRAINS
1900-1914 (I)

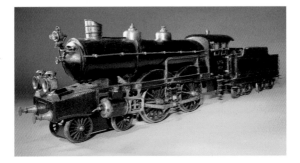

A Märklin live steam German-outline 'Württemberg' 4-4-0 locomotive and an 8-wheel American-style bogie tender; 1914; Gauge III; value code B

Identification checklist for Märklin Trains 1900-1914
1. Does the train have a mechanism, either electric, clockwork or live steam?
2. Does it have a clear maker's mark?
3. Is it of good quality?
4. Does it have a distinctive Märklin coupling?
5. Does it have a thickly lacquered finish?
6. Does the livery identify for which country or company the train was made (see below)?
7. Is it of heavy gauge tinplate?

Märklin trains
Having taken the lead in train production at the Leipzig toy fair in 1891 by introducing a regular system of gauges (see p.176), Märklin moved into the 20thC with a series of increasingly realistic locomotive models and an ever larger range of rolling stock, stations and accessories.

The 'Württemberg' in the main pictures was made in 1914 and is an excellent example of how much Märklin's trains had developed since 1900, from simple four-coupled clockwork locomotives to realistic and well-detailed trains.

Gauges
This clockwork tank locomotive (below) was made in 1900 in the new '0' Gauge, first used in 1891, but not universally found until around the turn of the century.

Although it is much more sophisticated in design than some contemporary trains, with deep splashers over the wheels, it still has crude leading wheels with infilled spokes.
* Note the carriage behind. It is an interesting and unusual verandah car specially designed for passengers to be able to admire the landscape.

This early live steam Gauge II locomotive (below) is an example from c.1900. It is rare, partly because it was remarkably dangerous and was in production for a short time only.
* The fuel reservoir in the tender feeds a combustion chamber under the cab roof, which blasts a jet of flame along the inside of the boiler to produce steam.

Coupling

The couplings on trains are a good way of dating Märklin trains. Early trains, such as the tank locomotive (below) used a tin loop; from 1904-1909, onwards they had a hook and, between 1913 and 1954, they used a sliding drop link.

Accessories

Märklin also developed and enlarged their range of rolling stock and accessories to complement their trains.

This Dutch market 'Centraal' Station (above), made c. 1904 is typical of the accessories available. The paintwork is of good quality and there is great attention to detail – note the decoration on the roof.
* Other accessories include bridges, such as the one at the top of the page.

Mechanisms

By the early 20thC, most trains were mechanised, making them more appealing to children. Two methods were used: either live steam, which was messy and potentially hazardous, or clockwork, which was safe but tiresome.

Märklin introduced electric motors in 1898, and by 1900 had several different alternating current designs, including four-volt, eight-volt and the potentially dangerous 110-250 volt. These different voltages were necessary to cope with the varied systems of AC/DC current available in Europe at the time, when there was no unitary electricity system.

The 'Charles Dickens' 2-4-0 locomotive (below) is typical of the type of electric locomotive produced c.1902. Distinctive features include:
* Heavy plated outside motor frames to carry the end bearings, which have been designed to imitate coupling rods.

MÄRKLIN TRAINS
1900-1914 (II)

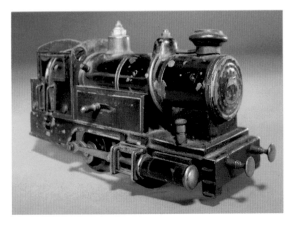

Märklin's overseas market

As the greatest toy train company of this period, Märklin was always keen to tailor its production to the appropriate export market. The German-outline 'Württemberg' locomotive (p.48) is here coupled to an American-outline tender; the 'Charles Dickens' (p.49) was made for the British market, but, despite the name, still retains a typical Germanic outline and six-wheel tender.

Swiss market

This is a rare Alpine rack railway-summer coach c.1904 (below), including details such as delicately painted rows of curtains.

American market

Locomotives for the American market generally stayed the same in shape as the German outline, with a cowcatcher attached as a concession to American taste, which can be seen in this one (bottom) made c.1902.

The coaches belonging to the train feature ungainly, standard-sized, clerestory roofs on short-ened coach bodies to imitate the typical American double-ended open verandah car.

British market

At the height of its imperial power, Britain, one of the wealthiest European countries at this time, represented an unrivalled potential market place for quality German toys.

One of the key figures in Britain's toy industry was Wenman Bassett-Lowke. A born entrepreneur, he started a successful mail order toy and model catalogue in 1899. Although synonymous with British trains, he had most of his stock made overseas by Bing (see p.54) and faced very little competi-

'Decapod' 10-wheel Great Eastern tank locomotive.
* In spite of successes, Gauge III locomotives were to prove too large for the British market and by 1910 only '0' Gauge and Gauge I trains were accepted by the London store, Gamages.

Prior to the outbreak of war, in 1914, Märklin continued to modernise its range in Britain with mixed success. But, it still failed to supply Bassett-Lowke regularly and so concentrated on streamlining its home production.

tion. in Britain. Märklin countered this firm grip on the market by manufacturing a large proportion of their exported material for A.W. Gamage, proprietor of the famous toy store in High Holborn, London. Neither man openly admitted the source, although Gamage did acknowledge the word 'Foreign'.

Märklin represented all the major British railway companies in their toy trains, with some companies modelled more frequently than others.

This early live steam Gauge I LNWR (London & North Western Railway) locomotive and tender (above) dates from c.1902. Apart from the splashers and tender lettering, it bears very little resemblance to the prototype locomotive, but it did help to pave the way for such rarities as the locomotive and tender at the bottom of the page.

One of the finest examples of Märklin's specialised production for the British market is this live-steam '0' Gauge 0-4-0 tank locomotive c.1905 (main picture). Finished in the rarely seen dark blue livery of the Great Eastern Railway, this locomotive remains extremely sought after.

The livery is the most accurate feature, for, despite having only four wheels, it represents the

Collecting
Märklin trains have the highest status in toy collecting, reflected by their values, which are in a similar bracket. This German-outline 'Süd Express' saloon coach from the Royal Train, c.1909 (below) is a superb example of a detailed, colourful, but restrained

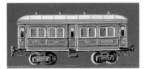

toy. It even shows the rings for the window blind pulls. Stock from the Royal Train is highly valued by collectors.

Although frequently outsmarted by other manufacturers, such as Bing, the solidity of their products represents their longevity – Bing collapsed in 1933, while Märklin still thrives today.

It is likely that the value of Märklin's older trains will always appreciate and can be considered a solid investment.

Variations
Of similar dimensions to the massive 'Württemberg' locomotive (p.48), this Gauge III (75mm) LNWR train (below) was made c.1904, again specifically for the British market and has

many characteristics typical of Märklin in this period:
* powerful live-steam mechanism
* many detailed features and solid construction
* coaches with hinged fall-plates between them.

BING TRAINS 1900-1914

*A clockwork 'King Edward' locomotive and tender;
c.1905; Gauge IV; value code C*

Identification checklist for Bing Trains 1900-1914
1. Is the train loosely based on a contemporary model?
2. Does it have a Bing's maker's plate?
3. Is the paintwork original?
4. Is the paint thinly, but finely, applied?
5. Does it have a solid construction?
6. Are the coupling rods plain?
7. Does it have a mechanism, either early clockwork or later electric?

Bing trains
By 1900 Bing were at the peak of their rivalry with Märklin and other, smaller, German toymakers. As Märklin had already managed to capture the top end of the market, in spite of their efforts, Bing decided to increase their development of mass production. By taking a more adventurous, modern and machine-orientated approach to manufacture between 1900 and 1914, they were able to develop a wide range of popular toy trains.

Technique
Bing's trains varied greatly in price and quality, from simple lightweight, lithographed tinplate coaches with ungainly locomotives to better-quality models, such as the 'King Edward' in the main picture, made using their new techniques. This involved lithographically printing flat sheets of tinplate with some hand-painting added later. The sheets were then folded, giving the tinplate strength but keeping it lightweight.
* If similar locomotives are compared, Märklin's are more sturdily soldered and have thicker paint-

work and lacquering, which tends to shrink and craze slightly more than Bing's thinly, but finely, applied paintwork.
* Bing's method of production was copied by other German makers, such as Carette, Karl Bub and Kraus, and came to be known as the 'Nuremberg style'.
* Note the crispness of the lining: on most Bing locomotives liveries were lined with either red, green or black.
* Bing's flexible production methods made it easy for them to adapt their trains for the overseas markets. The 'King Edward' is in British outline.
* The 'King Edward' is also a good example of how Bing's trains gradually modernised over this period.
    It combines an old locomotive, with a narrow smoke box and boiler, widely spaced and out-of-scale cylinders, with later features such as a well-proportioned cab and tender.
* As Great Britain was one of the most important overseas markets for German toy manufacturers during this period, Gebrüder Bing designed many of their trains in British outline.

Passenger stock

Bing's passenger stock was often far more colourful than their locomotives. This passenger coach (above) is a German-outline model of a French coach to run on German rails.
* Note the undersized bogies, reflecting Bing's lack of attention to realistic detail; however, the scale-length of the bogies is usually more accurate.
* The drooping corridor connectors were added later.

Germany

Bing's domestic market, was naturally a very important source of revenue for Bing, particularly as they were fierce rivals with their main competitors, Märklin.

The standard of both companies was so high that it was often very difficult to differentiate between them.

America

Although America had its own toy train industry (see p.57) many European companies were keen to break into this enormous market too. Bing were one of the most successful, as they were

able to offer better quality trains than were available already in the United States of America.

This one (below) is an example of an inexpensive 4-4-0 locomotive and tender made c.1905:
* It has a cast-iron body – a popular material for toys in America.
* The tender coupling has been replaced with one by Märklin.
* Note the distinctive American cow catcher – Bing tried hard to represent real American trains – and the Gebrüder Bing brand name prominently displayed on the side of the cab.

Collecting

Bing's trains are highly sought after by collectors, as they represent some of the most interesting toy trains produced. Condition is of importance and damage will lower the value, and it is crucial to have the complete, original locomotive and stock – look carefully for parts, such as coupling rods, which may have been added later, or replaced parts. Repainting reduces value too and is particularly common on spirit-fired steam locomotives.

France

Bing tried to develop business in France, but found it hard as France produced its own models. One of Bing's most successful trains was this 'steeple-cab' electric-outline locomotive (right), made c.1912.

BASSETT-LOWKE
TRAINS 1900-1914

A Bing for Bassett-Lowke 'Precursor' LNWR tank locomotive; c.1911;
Gauge I; value code E

Identification checklist for Bing trains made for Bassett-Lowke 1900-1914
1. Is the train accurately modelled?
2. Has it been designed after a British locomotive?
3. Is the paintwork complete, with full original livery and lining?
4. Does the train have a typical Bing coupling?
5. Does the mechanism work?

Bassett-Lowke (1899-present)
Unlike his contemporary, Frank Hornby, British entrepreneur and businessman Wenman Bassett-Lowke, did not enjoy manufacturing toys, preferring to subcontract design work and toymaking. In 1899 he started a mail order catalogue selling locomotive and steam engine components. A successful partnership began when Stefan Bing and Wenman Bassett-Lowke met at the Paris Exhibition in 1900. Realising the potential marketplace in Britain for Bing's expensive quality toy trains, Bassett-Lowke proceeded to combine the design skill of his business colleague, Henry Greenly, with Bing's manufacturing ability, to produce a range of highly successful locomotives over the next 15 years.

Bing for Bassett-Lowke
The LNWR 'Precursor' tank locomotive in the main picture was first made for Bassett-Lowke by Bing in 1911 and continued to be made well into the 1920s. It is therefore fairly easy to find today, and makes a good layout workhorse, as the real prototype did.
   Of the many locomotives made by Bing for Bassett-Lowke in this period, one of the best-known is the live-steam 'Black Prince' locomotive. It was available in three gauges: this one (opposite centre) is the largest, in Gauge III, and was fitted with a range of features:
* brass boiler
* tender with embossed frames and imitation springs
* double-acting cylinders
* reversing motion
* water gauge

Regional variations

To satisfy the British demand for regional variations, Bing produced trains in the liveries of all British railway companies. However, to save money, basic standard parts such as cylinders, remained the same in these trains.

The 'City of Bath' (above) was made c.1912. It has a distinctive sandwich frame, with bearings and springs visible outside the wheels, not within, as later was to become common practice.
* Note also the coupling rods ouside the splashers and the side frames on the tender.

'County of Northampton'

The 'County of Northampton' locomotive (opposite, centre) was made in 1910 and is an impressive and accurate representation of a genuine railway engine.
* Note how it includes the distinctive Great Western safety valve cover.

Collecting

The variety and quality of trains made for Bassett-Lowke means they are desirable and among the more highly valued trains, yet can be found very easily.

Accessories

Bing also provided Bassett-Lowke with a range of expensive and well-made accessories, including track signals, lineside buildings and miniature advertising signs (often promoting either Bing or Bassett-Lowke).
* This tinplate station (below) for Gauge '0' trains is made of lithographed tinplate and comes complete with electric lighting, a novel feature for this period.
* Note the fine quality of detailing, such as the window frames.

Carette

Other important suppliers to Bassett-Lowke were Carette. As well as making locomotives, Carette also produced a range of lithographed tinplate Gauge I freight stock, such as these (below), which include a promotional Bassett-Lowke wagon, c.1912, representing some of the finest lithography ever seen on British-outline rolling stock.
* In 1917 Carette sadly went out of business and several companies, including Bassett-Lowke, bought their tooling to use in their production.

Pre-war Carette parts are therefore commonly found on post-World War II Bassett-Lowke trains, but they will always carry different lithography.

OTHER TRAIN MAKERS
1900-1914

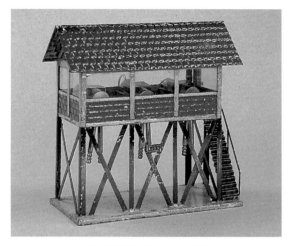

A Rock & Gräner signal cabin; c.1900;
10in (25cm) long; value code F

Note: The range of trains is so vast and varied, that it is not possible to provide a single, definitive checklist.

Rock & Gräner (1813-1904)
Rock & Gräner trains were of a very high quality and their attention to detail pre-empted that of other leading makers, such as Märklin and Bing.

There produced a series of fine locomotives and stock, as well as a range of buildings and accessories, such as the signal cabin in the main picture.
* The cabin is ingeniously fitted with three pneumatic levers, which are connected by rubber hoses to the appropriate points and signals, operating them all in correct synchronisation.
* They also made a famous

'Armoured Train', as used in the Boer War, with spring-firing guns on two of the wagons – typical of Rock & Gräner's attention to detail – and a rifleman's wagon at the back.

Schönner (1875-1910)
Having led the way with the development of the first steam engine toy in the late 19thC, Schönner quickly progressed to making good-quality and well-detailed trains, such as this South East & Chatham Railway 4-4-0 locomotive and tender (below).
* This one has been restored and repainted. Originally, it was made

using a finish that consisted of applying large printed transfers over a hand-enamelled finish.

Despite Schönner's high standard of workmanship, the company closed in 1910, even though their toys were briefly marketed by Bassett-Lowke and appear in their 1905 catalogue. Consequently, their trains are highly sought after today.

Carette (1876-1917)

Carette produced a range of finely built locomotives in addition to their other toys (see p.36), but they did not have the strength and durability of either Märklin or Bing's toys.

Founded by Georges Carette, a Frenchman based in Germany, the company flourished until the outbreak of World War I, reaching the zenith of its production with its trains made for Bassett-Lowke (see p.55). With the outbreak of war, Carette left Germany in 1914 and the firm was closed in 1917.

In its own right, Carette produced a range of locomotives for the American market, such as the Baldwin Vauclain Compound 4-4-0 locomotive (below) c.1905.
* The most common of Carette's own brand of locomotive is the inexpensive 'stork-leg' range, so-called because of its curious wheel arrangement, with two undersize wheels at the front and a pair of very large driving wheels with simple oscillating cylinders.

Other makers
* Other companies included Issmayer, Lütz, Hess and Plank, which all made cheaper, lightweight, coloured, gilded and lithographed tinplate toys and trains, similar in style to penny toys. Plank also made sturdier, live-steam locomotives, including the popular 0-4-0 'Vulkan'.

One of the few British toy train makers that briefly flourished were James Carson & Co. Ltd., which operated from 1900-c.1913 and then were absorbed into Bassett-Lowke.
* Identifiable by the large number of components used, particularly of chassis parts (most trains were made from only a few pieces of folded metal).

'Dribblers' and 'piddlers'

Usually made of brass by manufacturers such as Clyde Model Dockyard in Glasgow or Stevens Model Dockyard in London, these locomotives, such as this one made by Stevens c.1900 (bottom), were so-named because they had a live-steam mechanism, were of simple construction and had a 'dribbling' motion. First produced c.1870, they were made until the 1920s when Model Dockyard finally became retailers for other, more successful, makers:
* Features include three radially-set axles causing it to run permanently around in circles.
*A tall spectacle plate (the cab front that protected the driver).

America

The American market for trains continued separately from Europe, along with the rest of their toy industry. However, manufacturers quickly learned from German success and Ives, Carlisle, Finch and Voltamp and Lionel made trains in the European style.

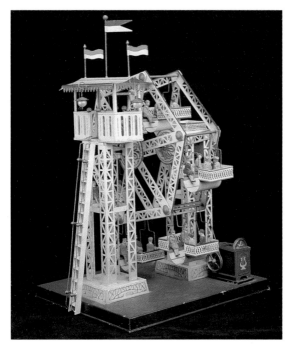

A Doll & Cie fairground wheel, c.1925

Once the major toymakers had recovered from the effects of World War I, the inter-war period became an exciting time for toy production, with new makers and a wider choice of toys available to suit all pockets.

Immediately after the end of the war Germany was still the world leader in toy production, particularly for export. The huge economic problems Germany faced had led to casualties however, and Carette closed in 1917. Other companies bought up their tooling so it is possible to recognise Carette parts in toys made by Bing and Bub.

However, Bing did not manage to survive for much longer either. The hyper inflation in Germany from 1922 onwards combined with the effects of the Wall Street Crash in America in 1929 led to the closure of Gebrüder Bing in 1933. The Bing family left Germany after the closure, owing to the political pressures there, and moved to England, where they later started up the company, Trix, in association with Bassett-Lowke, producing a highly successful range of '00' Gauge toy trains (see p.150).

After the extravagances of the Edwardian period, when there was a ready market in Europe for expensive quality tinplate toys, this period saw makers adapt to the new social order and produce less expensive toys. In order to do this, it was necessary to simplify production techniques. The quality of Bing's lithography deteriorated rapidly in the late 1920s. Lehmann, another established firm, produced a colourful and attractive range of novelty figures, now rivalled by the rising firm, Schuco, considered by many to be the most exciting toymakers of the 20thC. The makers, Günthermann and Stock also enjoyed success.

Wooden toys continued to be a central European speciality, with many inexpensive but well-made items produced for export to countries such as England and France. Wooden toymakers thrived in Britain too. One of the most famous firms was Forest Toys of Brockenhurst, named after the village in the New Forest in Hampshire, England, where the company was based.

Britain saw a prolific period of toy production; Meccano, the construction sets invented by Frank Hornby at the turn of the century were now at the peak of their popularity. The range also including chemistry sets, dolls' houses and electric experimentation sets.

The other major successes of this period for Hornby were the new diecast Dinky Toys (see p.110) and the popular Hornby Series railway system (see p.88). Other important makers of this period include Burnett, Chad Valley, Wells o' London and Brimtoy.

Other European countries were enjoying successes too. In France Fernand Martin made toys based on characters found in everyday life, succeeded by Victor Bonnet, while C.I.J. concentrated on well-made racing cars and making cars for André Citröen. Some high-quality toys were also made in Italy and Spain, which are mainly collected today in the country of origin.

In America the toy industry continued to develop independently. In addition to producing toys for the domestic market, it also became a strong exporter, with makers such as Lionel Corporation and Louis Marx soon household names across Europe.

It can be argued that the toymaking industry became more sophisticated during this period too, as makers woke up to the opportunities available in mechandising popular characters, such as Pip, Squeak and Wilfred from the Daily Mirror cartoon strip, Bonzo, Felix the Cat as well as Mickey Mouse and other characters from Walt Disney's hugely popular cartoons.

Similarly, the British biscuit tin industry continued to flourish, with new designs produced in interesting vehicle and aircraft forms.

Sadly, it was at the peak of success, in late 1939, that war once again put a stop to production. All toy production ceased in Britain in 1940 and factories were turned over to producing munitions. By 1941 it was even illegal to trade in toys. Toy production did not properly restart until well after the end of World War II, by which time, yet again, the market place had been transformed.

CARS & MILITARY VEHICLES 1918-1940

A rare pre-World War II two-tone Schuco Radio-Auto 5000;
c.1938-43; 7in (27cm) long; value code D

Identification checklist for Schuco vehicles 1918-1940
1. Is the vehicle marked 'Made in Germany'?
2. Is it made from both lithographed and painted tinplate?
3. Is it of good quality?
4. Does it have a clockwork mechanism?
5. Is it streamlined in design?
6. Does the vehicle have good-quality rubber tyres?

Schuco (Schreyer & Co) (1912-1978)
Based in Nuremberg, Schuco became well-known for novelty toys, cars, soft toys, boats, aircraft, clockwork animals and (in the 1960s) for its diecast cars.

As with many companies after World War I, Schuco's toys were made in large quantities to reach a wider market and reduce production costs. However, their toys still maintained a high quality, with a glossy paint finish and good-quality rubber tyres.

This ingenious Radio-Auto in the main picture was very popular in the late inter-war period. A musical toy car, it is able to play a popular contemporary German tune while driving along at the same time!

The car's aerial is an On/Off switch for the music, and under the bumper is a switch to control the driving mechanism of the car.

* Two-tone colours were a popular design feature on top-of-the-range cars in this era and this toy was made in three variations: blue with navy blue; red with maroon; and cream with maroon.

Technique
Schuco's toys were always very well designed and were often based on elegant contemporary models. The streamlined shell of the toy is a one-piece pressing, with a separately tabbed base plate. Any chrome additional parts, such as bumpers, were tightly fitted on to the main shell, preventing any sharp corners.

Boxes
All Schuco vehicles were sold in attractive boxes, such as the one in the main picture.
* This toy also came with well-illustrated instructions written in several languages.

Bing

Bing's toys were not made with so much detail during the inter-war period as they had been before and were often more flimsy in construction too.

This painted tinplate clockwork Ford Model 'T' six light (window) saloon car (above) represents a contemporary popular Ford and is typical of the cheaper end of their range.

Märklin

Although Märklin is best-known for their trains during this period, they also achieved success with tinplate car construction kits in the 1930s, such as this one for a streamlined saloon car (below), in competition with Meccano in England (se p.68).

Main features of these outfits:
* glossily painted and durable tin-plate components – necessary as cars were frequently taken apart and put together again
* easy to construct
* made loosely to represent contemporary vehicles including a streamlined saloon car, a petrol tanker and a racing car.
* colourful box, with good-quality and attractive illustrations.

Before buying the body of a vehicle, it was necessary to buy a beginner's set comprising a standard turquoise-coloured chassis, which fitted all cars.

Distler (1900-c.1960)

Well-known for their small, affordable tinplate toys, this six-light saloon car made c.1930 (below) is a typical example from their inter-war range of vehicles:
* It is made from good-quality lithographed tinplate.
* The car features an electrically-lit front indicator and brake light and open-flap windscreen.

* The number plate bears the initials of the company, 'J.D.N' (Johann Distler, Nuremberg)
* However, this example (below) is particularly unusual, as the car is driven by a lithographed tin-plate chauffeur.

Military vehicles

Military toys were usually accurately based on contemporary transport to recreate realistic battle scenes, and were modelled to the highest standard. The chief makers of these toys were from Germany (which also exported toys to other countries) and include: Hausser, Lineol and Tippco, who made this camouflage finish lithographed tinplate German Army ambulance (left) in the late 1930s.
* Note the composition driver – it is common to find such figures accompanying tinplate vehicles.

LINERS & OTHER BOATS
1918 - 1940

A fine clockwork painted tinplate, twin screw, third series liner, 1925; 24in (63cm) long; value code C

Identification checklist for Bing liners 1918-1940
1. Is the boat made of painted tinplate?
2. Are the portholes stamped on?
3. Is the vessel solidly built?
4. Does the hull have two soldered sections joined with a seam?
5. Is the boat complete, with all the deck fittings?
6. Does the boat represent a contemporary liner?
7. Is the deck removable?
8. Does the boat have Bing's maker's mark printed on the rear of the deck?

Bing boats
After World War I, Bing's boats, in common with most toys, were made of fewer components, some of which were now lithographed rather than hand-painted. As a result, they were simpler, but still some of the best toys available.

The boat in the main picture is one of the largest in a series of liners (the value rising accordingly), and is typical of Bing's post-World War I production for the following reasons:
* It is well-detailed. The larger the vessel, the more detail and realism was added.
* The boat has a clockwork mechanism, which increasingly replaced the use of live steam.
* It is without its original box – boxes rarely survive as boats were not always dried after use and would rot the boxes.

* It was made for an overseas market: Bing made boats for different countries, displaying their national flag, in this example the Union Jack for Britain. Otherwise, the boats have the same construction.
* The design of the boat was loosely based on the elegant liners of the period, an era when travelling abroad by ship was extremely fashionable.

Märklin
Although Bing was the most prolific German boat producer during this era, other makers, such as Märklin, Fleischmann and Arnold also made some highly collectable ships and boats.

This hand-painted liner (top right) was made by Märklin c. 1919. Although it is in poor condition, it is still very desirable and

has many features typical of all Märklin's boats from this period:
* Powered by live steam – this was gradually phased out and replaced by cheaper clockwork
* It is full of detail, such as simulated planked decks, an adjustable rudder, ventilators, hatch covers and covered walkways. However, this one is missing some features, such as masts and some lifeboats.

Submarines

As submarines were made as underwater toys, they were easily lost in ponds and lakes and have become extremely rare. They were particularly popular during the inter-war period as Germany improved and developed its range of U-boats.

This one (below), made in 1936, was one of the last water vessels produced by Märklin, and, as a military vessel, it has

many interesting qualities:
* stamped portholes
* painted firing guns
* keel made of lead
* made in two halves: the upper and lower halves are soldered firmly together
* a clockwork mechanism – lasting five minutes for this example – the keyhole in submarines is usually in the conning tower.
* action consisting of diving, moving underwater and returning to the surface, with moving hydroplanes.

Collecting

Boats from this period show a gradual decline in quality as makers, spurred on by the need to produce larger quantities, cut back on detail and production costs. However, these boats are still very collectable and fetch high prices.

Japan

Enomoto (active mid-20thC) made this clockwork Kaigun (navy) boat. As with many Japanese boats from this period, it is simple in construction and

streamlined in appearance.
* Pre-war Japanese toys are seldom seen and boats are some of the rarest. More individual in design than their mass-produced post-war toys, they are very desirable.

AIRCRAFT 1918-1940

A F.R.O.G. Hawker Hind biplane RAF trainer;
c.1941; 19in (48cm) wing span; value code D

Identification checklist for British toy aircraft 1918-1940
1. Is the aeroplane based on contemporary aircraft (either civilian or military)?
2. If a military plane, does it have a gun?
3. Is it lightweight in construction?
4. Does it have a rubber-band mechanism?
5. Is the plane still in its original box?
6. Is the plane made of a thin alloy frame covered with paper and aluminium (see below)?

Aircraft
The inter-war period was a boom era for toy aircraft. Toy planes and airships reflected contemporary developments occurring in actual civilian and military aircraft technology and models were made of both the new generation of fighter planes produced in the 1930s, and the luxurious civilian aircraft used for transatlantic flights.

Military aircraft
Toy planes were mostly marketed at older children, in the 10-15 age bracket, as they were often fragile and needed careful handling. Nearly all aircraft were based on real ones and would feature a wealth of accurate detail. The aeroplane in the main picture represents the Hawker Hind, a contemporary Royal Air Force training plane – note the registration number on the tail.

First bought in 1941, this toy had never been used and, remarkably, it still has the original instructions, packing note, oil bottles, rod, winder and band, all in the original box.
* All these extras help increase the value of a toy, but are often lost over the years.

Mechanisms
Toy planes rarely flew properly. Many had a simple rubber-band mechanism, which propelled them into the air for a few seconds, before plunging to the floor. Realistic appeal was achieved by other devices, such as: rotating propellers; motorised noises; and taxiing (moving along the ground).

Makers
One of the best-known British brands was F.R.O.G. (Flies Right off Ground) the trade name for International Model Aircraft Ltd, which were distributed by the firm, Lines Brothers.

* F.R.O.G. made many toy planes, which varied greatly in quality, such as the one in the main picture and this Hawker Hart Day Bomber (above).

The Hawker Hind was a limited edition adapted from the Hawker Hart and is more valuable, but otherwise they are very similar.

Technique
As with many toy planes, these two Hawkers were made from card, covering an alloy frame. This made them light, but fragile and prone to damage. The Hawker Hart has a crumpled top wing; it is rare to find planes without any damage and it lowers the value only slightly. Unlike others, they flew superbly.
*Aircraft were made in tinplate, too, such as Märklin's Lüfthansa Junkers JU90 (bottom).

Japan
It is rare to find pre-World War II Japanese toy aircraft, as they were made in small numbers only, specifically for the export market. This one (below) is a

1930s 'Farman' which is marked with (CK), the trademark of Kuramochi, one of Japan's leading distributors. It is a clockwork lithographed tinplate aeroplane – after the war aeroplanes became battery operated – and is more brightly coloured than those made in Europe.
* Wings are detachable to fit in the box; note the chips in the centre of the plane.

Boxes
Pre-war boxes were made of plain, brown card, cheaply stapled together, with an applied label on the lid.

* Very often the lid label depicting the aircraft is unrepresentative of the toy inside the box.

Collecting
Toy aircraft of all types are far less easy to find today than toys such as boats and trains, partly because fewer have survived. Japanese toys are rare and are extremely sought after. European planes are popular too, with collectors looking for rare versions and aeroplanes still with their original boxes and parts.

Märklin
Märklin mainly concentrated on making boats and trains in this period and their aircraft, produced only in small numbers, are greatly sought after today.
'Der Grösse Dessauer' (below) is a painted tinplate civilian passenger aircraft by Märklin made c.1938, based on a real Lufthansa Junkers JU90, made in Dessau.
* This aircraft is really a model

and is a good example of how Märklin were to move towards accurate more life-like miniatures, rather than the earlier character toys aimed at children.
* Possibly made for a travel agent rather than for children, it is still highly collectable, but would be difficult to display, as it is 27in (69cm) long, with a wingspan of 35in (89cm) long (this example is missing the cockpit canopy).

LEHMANN TOYS
1918-1940

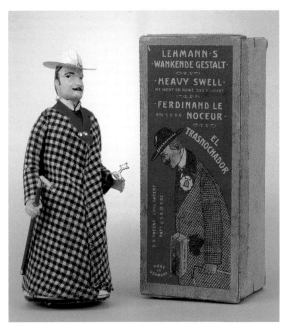

A rare Lehmann clockwork character, 'Heavy Swell';
23cm (9in) high; c.1918; value code C

Identification checklist for Lehmann toys 1918-1940
1. Is it a novelty toy?
2. Is the toy made of tinplate, either painted
or lithographed?
3. Does it have a wheeled undercarriage?
4. Is it lightweight, with fabric components?
5. Does it consist of many pieces, secured by tabs,
some of which are visible?
6. Is it of good quality?
7. Is it an imaginative design?
8. Does it have an integral key?
9. Is it in good condition (see below)?

Lehmann (1881-present)
Already well-established as
innovative toymakers by the
outbreak of World War I,
Lehmann continued to produce
high-quality mechanical novelty
toys after the war. Fortunately,
they were generally unaffected
by the major economic problems

Germany had at that time, as
many of their toys were sold
abroad. (Collectors can find
Lehmann toys fairly easily in
many European countries, as
well as in America.)

Ernst Lehmann continued
to be closely involved in all aspects
of design and production until he

retired in 1931. His keen eye for observing people's idiosyncrasies, already one of Lehmann's most famous hallmarks, is reflected in the character toy, 'Heavy Swell', in the main picture.

* Although its exact origin is unknown, the figure appears to represent a well-to-do gentleman – note the smart coat with brassy buttons and the hat and cane. It is possible too that the toy may be based on someone Lehmann knew; another clue is given in the name 'Ferdinand le Noceur' ('Ferdinand the Reveller') on the box, who may have been a well-known contemporary figure.

Colonial influence

Germany's involvement in East Africa from 1884 onwards fascinated Ernst Lehmann and the people, customs and animals from this continent were often reflected in his toys.

*The clockwork crocodile (above), complete with its original box, was made between 1898 and 1945, so it is difficult to date precisely. (Lehmann toys produced over a long period are less valuable than those made for only a short time.)

Nina, a cat and mouse toy (above), was made between 1927 and 1941. Following the Lehmann tradition, the toy cat is believed to have been named after a nursemaid who looked after the children of Johannes Richter, who took over the company when the founder, Ernst Lehmann retired.

* The cat has a simple, oscillating-mechanical device – the cat chases the mouse which appears to run away from it – and was aimed at young children.
* The cat was made with either green or yellow eyes.

Vehicles

In sharp contrast to makers such as Märklin and Bing, Lehmann's toy vehicles do not attempt to be accurate representations; the 'Tut-Tut' (below) is loosely based on a Tonneau (a popular style of car c.1900) and is possibly the most famous toy Lehmann ever made.

* First produced in 1903, the toy pokes fun at drivers who had to blow a horn regularly to warn other road users of their presence. The toy is fitted with real bellows and makes a realistic honking noise.

Condition

Lehmann toys are prone to rust, so check carefully before buying.

Collecting

With their ingenious designs and humorous appeal, these toys are highly sought after, with collectors preferring Lehmann designs which were made in short production runs.

MECCANO 1918-1940

Two No.2 Constructor and two Non-Constructor cars;
c.1934; value code E

Identification checklist for Meccano construction outfits 1918-1940
1. Are the components made of good-quality tinplate?
2. Are they painted?
3. Is the box made of top-quality cardboard, with an attractive, colourful label?
4. Does the kit include a complete set of tools and equipment (see below)?
5. Is the box marked with a number, from 0-10?
6. Does the set still have its original booklet of instructions?

Meccano (1901-present)
Meccano was founded in Liverpool by Frank Hornby in 1901 and was to become one of Britain's most important toy makers in the 20thC. Among their most well-known products were the successful range of Hornby trains (see p.88), the inexpensive and hugely popular diecast Dinky Toys (see p.110) and innovative, metal-strip construction sets (known as outfits).

Construction sets
Initially called 'Mechanics Made Easy', the early, pre-World War I sets were made of simple, unpainted, steel strips, followed by a nickel-plated version, in 1908, which could be constructed into a variety of models.
* The next big development was in 1926, when the first sets in red and green were produced.

Cars and aeroplanes
During the 1930s the range of constructor outfits was extended to include car and aeroplane sets.

Two constructor cars were available – the No. 1 constructor car could be built either as an open sports car, a coupé or a boat-tailed racer. The larger No. 2 constructor car was more complex – it was available with optional electric lighting, a hand brake and a diecast driver. The cars in the main picture depict some of the range: the ones on the left and right are No.2, while the central pair are non-constructor cars, much scarcer by comparison and worth three times as much.
   Aircraft construction outfits came in different sizes too, ranging from 00 (the easiest) to the more complicated No. 2 Special. The most commonly found are the No.1 sets, with blue and white parts, which construct a bi-plane.
* Note how the lid of the box of the one in the main picture depicts a much more modern plane than the actual toy.
* No. 2 outfits were able to make several different models.
* Clockwork motors were available for all kits at extra cost.

Other outfits

In addition to construction outfits, from 1935 onwards Meccano added racing and speed boats, chemistry sets, dolls' houses and electric sets, such as this rare Elektron Electrical Experiments Outfit No.1 (right) made c.1935.

Colour

From 1934-1940 the early type red and green finish (in different shades from postwar versions) was replaced by a blue and gold finish.

Tools and equipment

The quality of Meccano construction outfits was very high and care was taken to include all the necessary tools and equipment in each set. Complete, boxed outfits are very sought after and should contain the following components:

* screw driver
* spanner
* informative instructions
* an illustrated booklet describing the different models that can be constructed from each set.

Advertising signs

Meccano ephemera, such as catalogues, magazines and advertising signs are also collectable today. This selection of posters and display material (below) from the 1930s was originally used in shops and department stores to promote Meccano toys.

Collecting

Meccano toys are one of the most collectable British makes, particularly the rarer cars and oddities such as the 'Water Toy Duck'.

Boxes

Meccano's boxes were always made of top-quality cardboard with strengthened corners and an attractive, applied, coloured paper label. The inside of the box was fitted with a strong card, to which all the parts were tied.

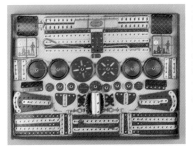

It is rare to find a completely intact box today, as once the models were assembled pieces were rarely taken apart and put back in the box. This complete wartime set (left) is particularly rare. It was made c. 1940-1941 and comprises parts for a vehicle kit, with plates, strips and rubber wheels.

OTHER BRITISH TOYS 1918-1940

A Triang Minic Rolls Royce; 1939;
4in (10cm) long; value code F

Identification checklist for Triang's Minic series 1935-1940

1. Is the toy pocket-sized?
2. Does it depict a contemporary, British vehicle?
3. Is it made of painted tinplate?
4. Does it have a clockwork mechanism?
5. Does it still have its original key?
6. Is it solidly made?
7. Does it have white tyres?
8. If a road vehicle, does it have a small petrol can fixed to the running board?
9. Does it have its original cardboard box?

Lines Bros. Ltd. (1919-1971)
The Lines family had first produced toys in the 19thC, primarily making rocking horses and other wooden toys. By the early 20thC their range had developed to include dolls' houses, toy prams and other, large, wooden toys. World War I interrupted their development, but in 1919, the three sons of the original founders, George and Joseph Lines, set up on their own. Their trademark was a triangle, symbolising the three partners, and they called their company Triang.

Their range comprised a variety of tinplate toys, soft toys, bicycles and scooters. One of their most successful products was an inexpensive range of pocket-sized clockwork cars, known as the Minic range.

Minic
Highly patriotic, these cars were always made to represent British vehicles, from industrial lorries and small Ford saloons to top-of-the-range Bentleys and Rolls

Royces (one is illustrated in the main picture). One of the most desirable was the taxi cab below, which was also produced in green, blue and yellow.
* More expensive versions came with features such as electric lighting and diecast passengers.
* Although these vehicles were well-made, be sure to check tyres before buying as they are prone to perishing.

Collecting
The inter-war period was a prolific era of production for these and many other British makers (including Wells o' London, Chad Valley and Burnett), and good

quality toys by well-respected makers are highly sought after. The success of the tinplate toy industry was complemented by that of the toy train market – this was achieved particularly successfully by Frank Hornby.

Toymakers were keenly aware that the market had matured since before World War I and developed the field at all levels, providing toys for all types and for all pockets.

In all, this is one of the peak collecting periods of British toys. It is also worth noting that, for many contemporary collectors, this era was also their childhood.

Mettoy (1936-1983)

Mettoy was founded in 1936 by Phillip Ullmann of Bechmann & Ullmann, successful toymakers in Nuremberg, who had fled Germany for Britain because of religious persecution.

Mettoy produced a range of inexpensive, lithographed tinplate toys, including this postal delivery van made in the late 1930s.

The van is not of the quality later associated with Mettoy after World War II: it is of flimsy construction and of a simple design. However, the slogans on the side add interest and would slightly increase the van's value.

Biscuit tins

Biscuit tins were already firmly established in Britain as popular toys (see p.45). This period saw the trend continuing, with more modern, novelty designs available. The two tins illustrated (below and top right) were made by the same maker, Barringer Wallis & Manners, but for different customers.

This tin (below) was made for the Co-operative Wholesale Society and advertises Crumpsall Cream Crackers.

Although it has suffered some damage to the roof and front bumper, it is worth more than the motorcycle, as there is better

detail in the lithography and it is fitted with electric head lamps.

Condition

Condition of biscuit tins is crucial. They are very prone to damage, particularly rust, and may were not cared for properly.

The motorcycle tin (above) was made c.1927 for Gray, Dunn & Co. Of lithographed tinplate, it has no mechanism and the motorcycle just freewheels. It is still in good condition, with no rust or noticeable decay.

OTHER EUROPEAN & AMERICAN TOYMAKERS

A Louis Marx 'Merry Makers', a clockwork, lithographed toy mouse band; c.1931; 6 ¼in (15.8cm); value code F

Note: The range of toys is so vast and varied that it is not possible to provide a single, definitive checklist.

America

The toy industry in the United States continued independently from Europe during the inter-war period. In addition to producing for the domestic market, it also became one of the world's leading exporters. Makers such as Louis Marx, Lionel Corporation and Kingsbury were soon well-known names across Europe.

Louis Marx (1920-1982)

Louis Marx became the largest toy manufacturer in the world by the 1930s, and even had a factory in England.

The 'Merry Makers' mouse band in the main picture is typical of the light-hearted, well-made and inexpensive tinplate toys Marx produced. The mice are made of folded and tabbed (see **Glossary**) pieces of tinplate, with simple, wire-like legs.

The piano has a clockwork mechanism inside, and, when wound, it enables the mice to move and play their instruments.

France

Two of the main makers in France were Fernand Martin (see p.26), which concentrated on toys based on characters found in everyday life and C.I.J. (Compagnie Industrielle de Jouets), which concentrated on quality racing cars, such as this Alfa Romeo P2 of c.1927 (below).

Made of painted tinplate, with a powerful clockwork mechanism, this racing car always carried the competition number '2'.

* It was made in different colours, representing the main European countries that competed in motor racing: silver for Germany; blue for France; red for Italy; green for Great Britain; and orange for Holland.

Germany
The toy companies that survived the war continued Germany's tradition of producing high quality toys that had helped the country remain the world leader in this field until World War II.

Schuco (Schreyer & Co 1912-1978)
This company is one of the most exciting novelty toymakers of the 20thC. This comic vehicle from the early 1930s (below) depicts a monkey driver holding a balloon.

Gebrüder Einfalt (1922-1935)
Einfalt also produced exciting toys, such as the amusing 'Embarrassed Girl' figure below.

* A good example of a novelty toy, the mechanism works when a lever is depressed by hand and the girl leaps off the chamber pot in surprise to reveal a mouse underneath the pot.

Günthermann (1887-1965)
Günthermann continued to be one of Germany's leading toymakers, producing a wide variety of clockwork tinplate toys, such as this appealing 'Tricky Ladybird', with a random circling mechanism, produced c.1920.
* Note the ladybird's very unrealistic antennae!

Italy
Italians made colourful and expressive toys. They are collectable today, although rarely found outside Italy.

Both these motorcycles (above) were made c.1932 by Ingap (Industria Nazionale Giocattoli Automatici Padua) and are typically Italian:
* They are made of thin tinplate.
* Brightly coloured; their clothing is flamboyant compared with similar pieces from other countries. The most commonly used colours are red, blue and yellow.

DISNEY TOYS 1928-1960

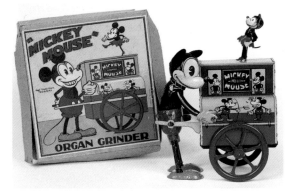

A lithographed tinplate clockwork organ grinder by Distler; c. 1931; 8 x 6in (20 x 15cm) square; value code A

Note: The range of Disney toys is so vast that it is not possible to provide a single, definitive checklist.

Licensing

The success of Mickey Mouse, the cheeky, lovable character first created by Walt Disney in 1928, led to one of the largest and most successful licensing phenomena ever known. Manufacturers competed energetically for licenses to produce Mickey Mouse and other popular Disney characters, and, by 1930, their production was well-established.

Until 1938 'Walt Disney Enterprises' or 'Walter E. Disney' usually appeared on German and American Disney Toys. British toys were marked 'Walt Disney Mickey Mouse Ltd'. In 1939 the name changed to Walt Disney Productions. The value of a toy is greater if the box confirms that it was made with the permission of the Walt Disney Company.

Tinplate Toys

German manufacturers were the first to be licensed to produce Mickey Mouse toys. This organ grinder by the Nuremberg firm of Johann Distler, made in 1931 (in the main picture), depicts an early version of Mickey turning the crank while a jointed tinplate Minnie dances to the tune produced by a musical box.
* This thin, toothy, rat-like Mickey is typical of many early

toys. Designers often worked from memory or simple sketches after seeing Disney films; as a result, many toys were inaccurate.
* This toy is extremely desirable and it is rare to see it in mint condition and with a box. Mickey Mouse's tail is missing, but this does not greatly affect the value.
* The golden age of Disney collectables was between 1928 and 1938. Important ones to look out for include: Mickey Mouse & Minnie on a motor-cycle by Tipp & Co., c. 1931; Mickey the Musical Mouse; and Mickey the Drummer, by Nifty.

Although Mickey Mouse is Disney's most famous and popular character, others, such as Pluto, Donald Duck and Goofy, were also represented. Made by Louis Marx in the 1950s the 'Goofy the Gardener' clockwork toy (below) is commonly available, but still

desirable. It is rare to see such a good example as this; the finish of lithographed tinplate clockwork toys wears off quickly.
* The most collectable Donald Duck figures are the early ones (pre-World War II), in which he has a long bill, including one made by Schuco.

Plastic
Marx, one of the largest toy companies in the world in the 1950s, were able to produce large numbers of toys cheaply by manufacturing them in Japan, where costs were lower.

Their Japanese division was called Linemar and they produced this tinplate and plastic clockwork Pinocchio (right) in the late 1950s.
* It is of much better quality than toys produced by Marx in America in the same period.
* It has many similarities to Japanese robot toys – it is of a similar shape, has a clockwork walking mechanism and is attractively coloured.
* It is very rare. (Pinocchio was less popular than Mickey Mouse and fewer examples were produced, so it is sought after today).

Other toys
* Amongst the many collectable Disney toys made between the 1930s and the 1950s was a Mickey and Minnie Mouse clockwork railway handcar. It was made in 1934 by the American firm, Lionel Corporation and was such an overwhelming success that it rescued the company from the threat of financial ruin.
* Lionel made the handcar in four colours: red; green; maroon; and orange. The maroon colour is the rarest.

Games
Games were another popular area used to promote Disney toys. This Mickey Mouse 'Tiddley Winks' game (below) is by the highly successful English firm, Chad Valley (1823-1978).

* It was made in the 1930s and is one of many games adapted by toymakers to capitalize on the popularity of Disney characters.
* Other popular Walt Disney games from this period include 'Pin the Tail on Mickey'.

Variations
This friction-powered lithographed tinplate toy called 'Mickey Mouse Mouseketeers Moving Van' was made by Linemar in Japan, c.1958:
* Linemar used one of their standard-issue lorries to make this toy, with Mickey Mouse, Minnie Mouse and Donald Duck printed on the side. The standard lorry was adapted to make several other versions too.
* The design of the lorry was loosely based on contemporary American models, indicating the important influence of American taste on Japanese toys in this era.

DISSECTED PUZZLES & JIGSAWS

'The Child's Own Clock', a coloured lithograph on wood dissected teaching puzzle by J.W.Barfoot; c.1860; 15 x 10in (38 x 25cm); value code H

Identification checklist for dissected puzzles 1800-1900

1. Is the puzzle brightly coloured?
2. Is it hand-painted and hand cut?
3. Does it have its original box?
4. Is there a label giving the name of the publisher and the date of publication?
5. Is the lithography or hand-colouring of good quality?

Dissected puzzles

The nursery played an important role in the lives of middle and upper-class children in the 19thC, as the centre for both education and recreation. Formal education, particularly for girls, was still rudimentary and would only take up part of the day and although playing with toys was permissible, high-minded Victorians believed recreation time was also meant to be spent profitably.

Consequently, dissected puzzles (later known as jigsaws) and board games (see overleaf), both educational and enjoyable, became increasingly popular pastimes for children.
* This early 19thC puzzle of 'The Child's Own Clock' in the main picture has many typical features of puzzles of this period:
* An educational theme: the puzzle introduces children to learning how to tell the time. Other popular subjects in the 19thC included scenes from the Bible or traditional stories, including 'The

Pilgrim's Progress' and 'Homes of England', as well as more light-hearted subjects, such as animals, nature and children's stories.
* The pictures (below) are from a double-sided, chromolithographic jigsaw puzzle depicting four scenes from the story, 'Robinson Crusoe'. It is in its original box and was sold together with a coloured booklet which showed how to do the puzzle, and also included a poem.
* Made from wood, hand-cut and hand-painted to a high standard.

This magnificent depiction of the Royal Coronation Procession by King George V and Queen Mary through Delhi in India in 1911 is an excellent example of the type of top-quality puzzle made for adults as an after-dinner amusement.
* The puzzle still has all the original pieces (essential when collecting), some are shaped into birds and other figures.

Makers

Puzzles were made by a variety of London-based printers and publishers. Some of the best-known 19thC makers include J.W. Barfoot, John Betts, Darton & Harvey, Milton Bradley in America, Raphael Tuck & Sons (1870-present), in addition to the Wallis family, who were also important makers of board games (see p.80).

Developments

By the early 20thC puzzles had changed in several ways:
* No longer hand-painted, pieces were now covered with chromolithograph-printed paper.
* Dissected puzzles began to be

called jigsaws, after the type of saw used to cut them.
* Card began to replace wood – it was cheaper to produce and cut more than one copy at a time.
* They were sold with the puzzle reproduced on the cover of the box, as illustrated in this early jig-saw (bottom left) by Chad Valley from c.1910, depicting a scene from 'Goldilocks and the Three Bears'. (Fairy stories and nursery rhymes were popular subjects in the first part of the century.)

Jigsaws often reflect the fashions and tastes of the era in which they were made – the quaintly dressed children in this 1930s 'Picture Building Puzzle' (above) by Raphael Tuck are reminiscent of characters in popular contemporary children's books.

Collecting

Although 19thC puzzles have been an established field for many years, puzzles made between 1900 and the 1950s have been largely ignored until recently, and it is still possible to find good-quality examples for just a few pounds. It is essential to choose those which still have the original box and all the pieces.

WOODEN TOYS 1900-1950

An acrobat and horse from the Humpty Dumpty Circus by Albert Schönhut; c.1910; value code F

Note: The range of toys is so vast and varied, that it is not possible to provide a single definitive checklist.

Albert Schönhut (1905-1935)

Albert Schönhut, one of the most important early 20thC American manufacturers of wooden toys, was born in Germany of a great toymaking family.

His toys are European in style. Perhaps the most well known is the Humpty Dumpty Circus, made between 1903 and 1935, featuring many performers, such as Hobo and Max & Moritz (German comic characters), a Chinaman, the acrobats in the main picture, as well as a large selection of different animals.
* Surviving Schönhut toys often need the rubber cords in their joints restrung, but this does not seriously reduce their value.
* Generally, Schönhut animals with glass eyes and circus artists with bisque heads and glass eyes are the most collectable.
* It is difficult to find a complete circus set and much easier and less expensive to collect individual Schönhut figures.

20thC wooden toys

Although Germany still produced large numbers of wooden toys during the first part of the 20thC, particularly from the well-established Erzegebirge region in Saxony, the major development this century was the growth of small wooden toymaking firms in Britain, especially in the period between the two World Wars.

* One of the best-quality English wooden toy firms was Forest Toys of Brockenhurst (1918-1939), named after the village in the New Forest, Hampshire, England where the company was based.

* It produced a wide variety of hand-carved and painted animals and figures, including this group of animals (opposite left), which are part of a large Noah's Ark set.

They have many features typical of these toys:
* The set is hand-painted.
* Pieces are chunkily built
* They are carved in flat planes.
* A contemporary catalogue from the 1930s states that 'the carving is so vigorous that Her Majesty the Queen remarked that 'they all looked so alive'. The catalogue also mentions that larger size dogs can be carved to resemble customers' own dogs and that photographs and portraits should be sent to obtain a good likeness!
* Brockenhurst produced several animal sets, such as types of nativity scenes, farmyards and hunting scenes.

Technique

Other major English wooden toymaking firms included Lines Brothers and Chad Valley, who made this colourful ark (below) in the 1950s. (These two firms made a wide variety of toys.)
* The figures are made of plywood and covered with coloured, printed paper.

Its simple design was fashionable at the time, but the quality of wood and the toy's overall appeal makes it much less desirable than the farm pictured below.

* This chunky wooden farm set was made in central Europe c.1930s (it is stamped 'Foreign'). Although the pieces have been crudely painted on a burnt-on design, it is charming and would still appeal to many young children and toddlers.

Yootha Rose

After World War II, a new development in toy design was the emergence of artist toy makers, who produced a wide range of attractive high-quality hand-made wooden toys.

After the horrors of wartime, aggressive toys, such as military vehicles, became less popular and there was renewed interest in traditional themes, such as farms and zoos, as well as Noah's Arks.

This cheerful carousel (above) was hand-made by Yootha Rose, a toy artist based in Sussex, England. Her trademarks were her colourful designs and the innovative use of household objects (the centre of this carousel is made from cotton reels!). Her expensive and decorative toys would often have been bought to look at and not to play with, so they can still be regularly found in good condition.
* Other important English toy artists from the 1950s through to the 1970s include Sam Smith and John Gould.
* Paul and Marjorie Abbatt were important manufacturers between the 1960s and 1970s producing a range of wooden, educational toys for under-5s, while John Galt's sturdy wooden toys were first produced in the 1960s and continue to be made today.

Collecting

Wooden toys vary enormously in value. At present, many pieces are still extremely undervalued and can be easily-bought for little expense at toy fairs, local markets and even jumble sales and charity shops.

BOARD GAMES 1800-1940

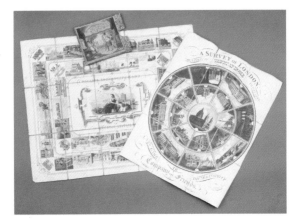

Left: 'A Survey of London' by William Darton, c. 1820; value code F. Right: 'Wallis's Loco Game of Railroad Adventure' by Wallis; 1840s; value code F

Identification checklist for board games 1800-1900
1. **Does the game still have its original slip case?**
2. **Does it still have its instructions?**
3. **Is the printing of good quality and brightly coloured?**
4. **Is the game made of paper mounted on canvas?**
5. **Is the subject of the game one of travel or a topical, contemporary event?**

Board games
The earliest board games date from the mid-18thC and were printed from copper or steel plates and coloured by hand. By 1839 lithography was first used, making it possible for publishers to produce larger quantities of all kinds of toys.

In common with dissected puzzles, games often then reflected contemporary preoccupations or are moral or educational in tone. The games in the main picture – 'A Survey of London' and 'Wallis's Loco Game of Railroad Adventure' have many features typical of 19thC board games:
* 'A Survey of London' depicts the city's most important buildings, while the 'Railroad Game' uses the newly invented steam engine as its central theme. Other popular subjects included contemporary events as well as historical, geographical, regional and educational subjects.
Typical features include:
* Simple rules – these two are

progressive games. Players move from the start to the finish as quickly as possible by taking it in turns to throw a pair of dice.
* Made of paper cut into sections and mounted on canvas, so it could be kept in a slipcase.
* A rectangular shape (you can also find round ones).

Makers
The 'Railroad Game' was made by Wallis (1775-1847), one of the most prolific British manufacturers of games and puzzles, and the 'Survey of London' was by William Dart (1755-1819), another important family company, best-known for their popular instructional games.

Other important 19thC makers include Brooks & Co. S. & J. Fuller, Thomas Varty, Carrington Bowles, Bowles & Carver and John Betts, which also produced puzzles, and Parker Brothers in America (1883-present). By the late 19thC games were mostly made by specialist makers, such as Jaques, Spears and Waddingtons, all of whom still produce games today.

Variations
Not all board games were flat. This 'Over the Garden Wall' game (below) from the 1880s is an imaginative version of tiddly winks. The aim is to flick the counters over the wall into the garden, scoring a different number of points depending on where they land:

* Made of solid lithographed card, the 'Over the Garden Wall' game was printed in Bavaria for the successful English games manufacturer, Spears.
Up until World War I many British companies regularly used Bavarian printers, as their work was of a high quality and extremely colourful – look for both the printers' and manufacturers' marks.
* The fountain and rose trees were made by the English firm, Britains; they later became world-famous for their toy soldiers and other figures.

Cycling was a popular pastime in the late 19th and early 20thC. The aim of this board game from 1890 (above) is a race to the finish and its light-hearted theme of avoiding mishaps on a cycle ride reflects the changing attitude to board games.
* By the 1890s games were mounted on folded board.
* Many new games were launched by the turn of the century, such as the perenially popular Ludo and Snakes & Ladders.

Following the successful development of the recently invented airship, air and even space travel were becoming exciting new fields of speculation. This 'Trip to Mars' game made c.1900 is an imaginative interpretation of outer space and would appeal both to games collectors and space enthusiasts.
* Made by unknown British manufacturers, this is a good example of a mass-produced game, which, although not high in quality, is very appealing.

Games 1914-1940
Board games during this period often took their inspiration from popular children's characters of the day. This Peter Rabbit game (below) by the publishers, Frederick Warne & Co., was based on the highly successful characters created by Beatrix

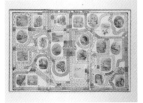

Potter in her children's story books. Published from 1917 onwards, the figures were originally made by Britains and were of high-quality hollow-cast lead. By the 1930s, however, these were replaced with plywood figures covered with printed paper.

Collecting
Condition is important; but rare, early games are always worth acquiring, even if slightly damaged. Look out for interesting subjects, such as travel or topical contemporary events, which are more appealing and more desirable than educational and moral games.

Hornby Series '0' Gauge accessories, c.1930

Train production slowly recovered after the end of World War I and, ironically, was once again at the peak of production by 1940, only to be destroyed by war again. World War I had had an enormous effect on society in general and, as a result, the market place for toy trains had drastically altered too.

The 'Homes Fit For Heroes' that British soldiers returned to were much smaller than ones built before the war and the massive Gauge I or II locomotives were no longer practicable or popular. In Germany, Bing quickly took advantage of their ability to produce lightweight lithographed tabbed tinplate trains (known as Nuremberg-style) and produced a range of locomotives and accessories at affordable prices and for all levels of the market. Märklin began to modernise their range too, although they continued to use a flatter, more traditional and heavy style, with soldered rather than tabbed joints.

Although German trains still dominated the market, the rise of patriotism meant that Britain was no longer the captive market it had been for German toys. Anti-German feeling was strong and the British manufacturers Hornby, caught the mood of the time by producing the slogan:

'British Toys for British Boys'. Companies such as Bassett-Lowke, which could not find supply from anywhere else but Germany, made great efforts to disguise the origin of their products, using the trademark, 'BW' (for Bing Werke) on all their product boxes.

These fundamental changes in the market place also allowed British companies to play a more important role. The most successful British company at this time were Hornby, which produced a new range of '0' Gauge trains in June 1920. Frank Hornby's original plan was to give these toy trains a simple nut and bolt construction (although with a special boiler and cab pressings), so they could be completely demountable.

These lightweight trains have a wonderful quality and great charm, but, as Hornby wanted to create more realistic models, the constructor concept was phased out from 1923. Hornby improved and developed their range during the 1920s particularly with their '0' Gauge range.

The inter-war period is extremely popular with train collectors and it is interesting to note how enthusiasts from train-producing countries have a natural affection for home-grown products.

Consequently, British collectors favour Hornby and Bassett-Lowke in particular. Hornby collectors have a wealth of choice and variety to choose from, as by the 1930s the range had grown to include a wealth of locomotives, coaches and freight stock, all complemented by Hornby Series farm animals set in countryside settings with Hornby Series trees and '0' Gauge scale Dinky Toys. There were also lineside accessories, such as bridges, signals, signal cabins and level crossings.

In sharp contrast, in Germany, in 1935, Märklin produced a range of massive eight-coupled locomotives, as well as railway stations measuring over 6ft (1.8m) in length. Track was made of solid steel and they also produced hand-painted and transferred accessories and an extensive range of coaches and freight stock, all in solid style.

In America, the Lionel Corporation continued to produce standard gauge railways. They were highly successful and Lionel were able to knock out many of their rivals.

The period between 1935 and 1940 was the consolidation of nearly 50 years of growing achievement by toy trainmakers, culminating in the manufacture of Märklin's final, magnificent 'Crocodile' (p.84) and Hornby's 'Princess Elizabeth' (p.92).

However, these '0' Gauge trains were soon to be superseded in popularity by smaller trains. In 1935, a new company, Trix, was founded by Stefan Bing, with a new '00' gauge range. In 1936 Märklin responded by producing their own version and, in Britain, in 1938, Hornby introduced their Hornby-Dublo range. Despite their small size, these trains were very well-made, more affordable and more convenient than '0' Gauge trains and were to became the most popular type of toy train for the next 50 years.

MÄRKLIN
1918-1940

A Märklin electric 'Crocodile' locomotive;
c.1937; Gauge I; value code A

Identification checklist for Märklin trains 1918-1940
1. Does the locomotive have a distinctive Märklin trademark and serial number?
2. Is the paintwork on the buffer beams or any other extremities original?
3. Are the pick-ups original and relatively unworn?
4. Is the finish detailed and of superb quality?
5. Is the locomotive an accurate representation of a real rail locomotive?
6. Is the train extremely solid and of heavy construction?
7. Does the locomotive have a twin electric mechanism?

Märklin trains
In 1918, after the end of World War I Märklin were quick to set about providing affordable and popular toy trains for all available markets. The Swiss-outline Gauge I 'Crocodile' locomotive in the main picture represents the zenith of Märklin's toy railway production in this period. By the date of manufacture, in 1937, Märklin's range had become so detailed and specialised that the trains were more like models.

* The 'Crocodile' also represents the extreme specialisation of Märklin's production, as the number of buyers who could have afforded this type of toy would have been limited.

Realism
Not all Märklin's trains were of this standard. Lower down the range, trains were often rather unrealistic in design, such as this Southern Railways 4-4-2 tank locomotive (below, left):

* Made in 1925, it is a weak attempt to produce a Southern Railway outline.
* Märklin's version of the famous 'Flying Scotsman' locomotive was equally curious, with a German-outline cab and grafted-on firebox sides.

Features

Models from the early part of this period still had some of the ungainly charm of the pre-war locomotive range, with heavy detailing in the tinplate construction, the lining and the painted features. This can be clearly seen in the Southern Railway 'Stephenson' 4-6-4 tank locomotives, c.1925 (above).
* Popular with European collectors as they shared a chassis with other models.

Gauges

These two trains (above) illustrate the difference in size and scale between '0' Gauge and Gauge I. Gauge I was too big to fit in the new houses built after World War I and became less popular. It is remarkable, however, that a commercial manufacturer such as Märklin was able successfully to produce such a large range of high-quality pieces.

Paint

The early 1920s paint finish usually has a pre-World War I sticky feel and tends to craze with age. By the 1930s, however, the paint was thinner and more smoothly applied.

Overseas markets

For the English market, a range of models was produced based on trains from the LNER, LMS, Southern and GWR companies:
* A popular series today, but hard to find in good condition.
* Because of the quality of the lacquer, which is finely applied and very smooth, they are particularly desirable.

Accessories

Concentrating mainly on the Deutsches Reichsbahn and Swiss and French outline locomotives, the revived range of accessories, included such items as street lamps and indicators, as well as various wagons, stations, newspaper kiosks and sheds.
* Buildings had less charm than pre-war models, and were generally plainer in finish. Märklin compensated for this by producing large composite buildings.

Late period

In 1933, Märklin created a range of six- and eight-coupled trains based on contemporary prestigious locomotives from different countries from around the world. These trains included the streamlined New York Central 'Commodore Vanderbilt', from North America, the German 'Borsig' locomotive and this grey and black 'Mountain Etat' French locomotive (below).
* The most desirable locomotives in this series for collectors are the green and black versions of the British London and North Eastern Railway 'Cock o' the North', which was made between 1935 and 1937.

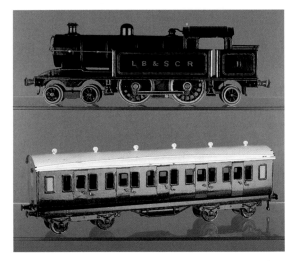

*A Bing for Bassett-Lowke electric LB and SCR Marsh tank locomotive and a
1921 Southern Railway coach, 1920; Gauge I; value code D*

Identification checklist for Bing trains 1918-1933
1. Is the locomotive marked (usually on the bunker back)?
2. Is the paintwork of high quality and delicately
applied, with a thin varnish on the surface?
3. Does the locomotive have flat couplings?
4. Does it have fluted coupling rods?
5. Is the coach lithographed with a painted roof or ends?
6. Is it Gauge I in scale (rather than '0' Gauge)?

Bing trains
The successful and seemingly
secure relationship between
Wenman Bassett-Lowke and the
Bing family first established in
1900 was much disturbed by the
effects of World War I. The market for model trains was more
sophisticated, but with people
living in smaller houses, greater
competition from other toy manufacturers and international
economic problems, they faced a
severe struggle to maintain their
position in the market place.

As Wenman Bassett-Lowke
was not primarily a manufacturer,
he was tied into his traditional
sources of supply. Although he
increasingly used the company
he founded before World War I
with George Winteringham (see
p.54), he was still tied to Bing for
much of his production.

In the nationalistic atmosphere
of the day, this connection was,
unsurprisingly, not always to his
liking, so Bing's name was rarely
flaunted in Britain.
* This reticence is confusing to
collectors, as Bing, as well as supplying Bassett-Lowke, also produced their own range of trains
for the bottom to middle end of
the British and German market.
* The '112' series of clockwork
and electric tank locomotives
were sturdy workhorse models
available in Gauge '0' or in
Gauge I, as is seen in this example (top of facing page).

Railway companies
In January 1923, Britain's various
railway companies were merged
into a simpler railway network
comprising: Great Western Railway
(GWR), London Midland &

Scottish (LMS), London and North Eastern Railway (LNER) and Southern Railway (SR).These changes had an enormous affect on toymakers' production and makers such as Bing quickly tried to adapt their trains to the new liveries.

The locomotive and carriage in the main picture illustrate the transition. The tank locomotive is a continuation of a pre-war model which continued well after World War I, while the coach has been adapted. Bing had produced a range of coaches for Bassett-Lowke in high-quality lithographed tinplate known as '1921 stock'. The events of 1923 rendered them antiquated, so a Great Western coach has been partly factory hand-painted over the original livery, on the sides and the roof, but with the end sections left untouched.
* It is extremely rare to find a coach of this period in such fine condition.

Freelance locomotives
Bing also produced their own range of 'freelance' locomotives, loosely modelled on contemporary British 4-4-0 locomotives with the same body shell in different liveries representing various railway companies.
* One of the most valuable locomotive of this series is the Southern Railways' 'King Arthur'.

Domestic market
This ungainly German outline electric windcutter 'Pacific' locomotive (below) is typical of the range produced by Bing for the domestic market.

Decline
In spite of some success overseas, the company declined, and by 1933 it had closed.

The Bing family moved to Britain and created a new company, Trix, in association with Bassett-Lowke (see p.150)

Accessories
Bing also produced an attractive range of tinplate accessories, such as stations.
* The ones on the left, which include platform lamps and station destination indicators, were made specifically for the English market.

HORNBY SERIES
1920-1930

*A Hornby Series No 3C 'Flying Scotsman' clockwork locomotive
and tender; c.1929-41; 'O' Gauge; value code F*

**Identification checklist for Hornby Series
trains 1920-1930**
1. Does the train have its original box?
2. Does the locomotive have a brass steam dome?
3. Does the locomotive have the early No.2 (not No.2
Special) tender?
4. Are the locomotive's wheels made of lead?
5. Does the locomotive have a drop-link coupling?
6. Are the locomotive and tender in their
original boxes?
7. Is the train made of tinplate?
8. Does it have a mechanism?

Hornby
In 1901 Frank Hornby had
invented 'Mechanics Made
Easy', a successful range of construction sets, which were
renamed Meccano in 1908 (see
p.68). At the end of World War I,
Hornby decided to extend the
Meccano principle to model railways. The early models were
very simple, comprising a set of
tracks, which had to be joined
together, and trains with thin
bodies, brass buffers and coupling hooks and thick-plated
wheels and axles. These early
locomotives had no identifying
livery and represented the pre-
1923 grouping of the Great
Northern, Midland and London
& North Western liveries.

Hornby Series
By 1923, Hornby realised that the
constructional features hindered
production and made the end
product look clumsy. As a result,
he developed more realistic
trains, such as the 1927 No.3C
'Flying Scotsman' in the main
picture. However, unlike Bassett-
Lowke, Hornby was not greatly
concerned with accuracy and the

trains had faults. For example,
the wheel arrangement is wrong:
it compresses the Sir Nigel
Gresley's 'Pacific' 4-6-2 wheel
arrangement to fit Hornby's No. 2
4-4-0 mechanism.
* Although of similar value to later
models, this early example has an
appealing toy-like charm which
was lost in later versions. Note
details such as the brass steam
dome, an attractive crest on the
cab side, an oversized coal rail and
an early style tender, carried over
from the constructional models.

One of the rarest and most
sought after items made by
Hornby during this period is the
first issue from the series of
Private Owner Vans, which were
made until 1941. Produced only
between 1923 and 1924, this rare
Colman's Mustard van (above)

clearly illustrates several typical early features:
* It has second-type nickel-plated wheels with thin axles.
* The van also has a second-type chassis with pierced axle guards. The supports for the first, thick-axle type were completely solid and were used between 1920 and 1922; the second type were used between 1922 and 1930.
* Note the Hornby Series transfer on the side frame too.

Boxes
The Hornby factory ensured that every item was packed in a sturdy, printed cardboard box. Boxes add greatly to the value of an item, as collectors have become more demanding.

They changed in design too, from a plain brown box (which would have been used for the Colman's van) to this, more typical, version (right) which was used until 1937.
* From 1937 the boxes carried useful date codes. The lettering changed to a sans serif typeface which was used until the 1950s.

One of Hornby's most successful products was a snow plough (below). It was first produced in 1924 and became plainer and simpler over the years.

This one, made c.1928-30, is distinguished by several features that were later dropped:
* sedate colour scheme (which later became blue and yellow, after 1933)
* sliding doors
* pierced axle guards
* lantern

Mechanisms
The electric No.1 Tank Locomotive (below) is an example of a transitional model. Powered by a six-volt DC permanent magnet motor, it is actually substantially safer than the first 'Metropolitan' railway set (above). It was introduced in 1925 at the time of the British Empire Exhibition and has an exciting, but potentially dangerous, high-voltage mechanism. Fortunately, later models became safer, but it is variations such as this early 'Metropolitan' locomotive which are most sought after by collectors today.
* The No.1 Tank Locomotive is an early electric example. Note how the electric mechanism sits uncomfortably with the brush caps sticking out in an ungainly way through the tank sides.
* The model was completely revised in 1931, making this version, complete with resistance controller, a rare find.

HORNBY SERIES 1930-1940

*A Hornby Series Southern Railway E120 Special tank
locomotive; 1935; 'O' Gauge; value code F*

Identification checklist for Hornby Series 1930-40
1. Does the locomotive have large 'Special' wheels?
2. Does the train carry a post-1923 British livery?
3. Is the train made of tinplate?
**4. Are the locomotive, tender and coaches all of a
high quality?**
5. Does the roof still have its original paintwork?
6. Are all the parts original?
7. Is it a rare version of a particular model?

Hornby in the 1930s
Although not as realistic or
sophisticated as later, post-World
War II models, trains from this
period are of a high quality and
are sought after by collectors
today.

The No. 2 series bogie coach
(below) is typical of their production at this time. It was Hornby's
closest attempt at a scale-length
coach and, although falling far
short of contemporary Märklin
examples, the quality of the
printing is extremely good.

* Hornby made many more side
corridor coaches than suburban
-type passenger coaches.
* Although Hornby made
coaches for all four British railway companies, fewer Southern
Railway ones were made and so
are most sought after.

Following the success of the
No.2 Southern Railway coach,
Hornby produced a revised version of the Southern Railways
E120 special tank locomotive
(in the main picture), also in
1935. It differs from the less

valuable No. 1 version with a chunky body and more realistically scaled wheels that run under the footplates. It was made in all four liveries. However, it is hard to find today, particularly in good condition, as it was made in relatively small quantities and was often heavily played.
* Hornby also made a larger No. 2 Special tank locomotive, with the same mechanism.

Boxed sets
Before World War II stopped all toy production in 1941, Hornby produced its finest model and one of the most valuable today.

Packed in a beautiful fitted wooden case, the 1937 LMS 'Princess Elizabeth' 4-6-2 locomotive and tender (below) captures the style of the original locomotive and is the only time that Hornby achieved a six-coupled mechanism in '0' Gauge.
* Early models are distinguished by the sans serif lettering on the box and the sand colour inside the cab, which was replaced by a maroon colour in 1938.
* Note how the firebox is misshapen and rises too high, compared with the actual locomotive.
* Check the locomotive carefully for metal fatigue on the buffers, wheels, tender, axle boxes and

cross heads and the tender coal chute. Although they can be replaced, fatigue or poorly fitted replacement parts can lower the value of a piece.
* Also, check the box; if it has ever become damp the plush lining can rot the paintwork where it makes contact.
* Other collectable items from this peak of production in the late 1930s include a range of buildings, signals, lamps, water towers and various stock, including the much sought-after Private Owner Vans and Tank Wagons.

French market
The success of the Hornby Series ran parallel with the success of Dinky Toys (p.117) in France.
* Hornby's French factory moved from Paris to Bobigny in the early 1930s from where it produced a wide range of models, specifically for the French market.

Collecting
Until only a few years ago Hornby Series trains were bought by enthusiasts and regularly used and played with. Today, collectors are mainly interested in Hornby Series trains that are in pristine condition and which they can display, as they are now much more highly valued.

Schools class 'Eton'
One of Hornby's finest 4-4-0 locomotives, the Southern Railway Schools Class 'Eton' (below) was based on the Bramham Moor Hunt class LNER locomotive with various details added, such as

distinctive sloping cab sides, necessary for the real, narrow tunnels at Hastings in Sussex.
* This attention to detail did not stretch as far as the tender, which does not have the correct canted sides.

OTHER TRAIN MAKERS 1918-1940

A Bassett-Lowke electric lithographed tinplate 'Flying Scotsman' LNER locomotive and tender; 1933; 'O' Gauge; value code E

Identification checklist for Bassett-Lowke trains 1918-1940
1. Is the body made of lithographed tinplate?
2. Does the train have its original mechanism?
3. Does it have an electric mechanism?
4. Is the original detailing unaltered?
5. Are the wheels original?
6. Are the couplings and buffers original?

Bassett-Lowke
At the end of World War I, Wenman Bassett-Lowke faced several problems. In the nationalistic atmosphere that followed the war, Bassett-Lowke was forced to conceal the fact that Bing, a German company, provided him with most of his products. He was able to do this by using the 'BW' trademark on the boxes only, rather than on the locomotives and stock. Bassett-Lowke's other problem was that his stock now looked antiquated, particularly after the regrouping of the four national railway companies in January 1923.

'Flying Scotsman'
The Flying Scotsman in the Imain picture represents the pinnacle of Bassett-Lowke's achievement during this period:
* Designed by the managing director of Bassett-Lowke, Robert Bindon-Blood.
* First produced in 1933, the model is a masterpiece of tin printing and an accurate representation of the real train.
* It has an electric mechanism.
* An 'O' Gauge locomotive.
* It pulls a rake of scale-length coaches designed by engineer Edward Exley for Bassett-Lowke.
* A six-coupled locomotive, its overall appearance is much finer and more impressive than that of rival models.
* The 'Flying Scotsman' remained a popular model well into the 1950s and is still sought-after today.

The 'Moguls'
As larger gauges became increasingly unpopular owing to limited funds and space after the war, Bassett-Lowke developed their own new models .
* The most important and successful were the live-steam 2-6-0 Mogul locomotives in the livery of all four companies, introduced in 1925.

* Bassett-Lowke also made good use of the stock sold off by Carette after they went bankupt in 1917. Hence, the 1921 clockwork Peckett Southern Tank locomotive (above) is extremely similar to Carette's 1907 model. Their parts can also be seen in other Bassett-Lowke pieces, including an attractive 12-wheel dining car.

Märklin for Basset-Lowke
The demise of Bing in 1933 (see p.86) forced Bassett-Lowke briefly to renew contact with Märklin. They produced four locomotives for Bassett-Lowke, including the last '0 Gauge locomotives to be produced in Germany for the British market, such as this version of the Southern Railway Schools Class locomotive, 'The Merchant Taylor's' (below) in 1934.
* Although it is a good representation of the real tender, the cab sides appear too upright, the wheels are undersized and the brush caps are too prominent.

The future of Bassett-Lowke lay with large sales of Winteringham's tin-printed trains and the production of unique locomotives, ships and display models made to special order. Ultimately, it was for the latter that the company became most famous.

Collecting
Bassett-Lowke adopted an ambivalent position among collectors, uncertain as to whether they are toys or models. As a result of this and the relatively small number of toys produced, the market is not as developed as for some makers.

Germany
Other German companies of importance at this time are Kibri, notable for concentrating on an attractive range of '0' Gauge accessories, Fandor and Karl Bub.

Britain
Such was the power of the established smaller makers, that few companies tried to compete in Britain. Among a handful who succeeded other than Bassett-Lowke were Stedman (later Leeds Model Co.) and Mills, which produced sturdy, mixed traffic locomotives (mostly tanks and short-haul), as well as a limited number of more prestigious express locomotives.
Bowman of Norfolk produced several live-steam 0-4-0 and 4-4-0 locomotives in the late 1920s and early 1930s, which are worth little today as they are usually damaged. However, their coaches and wagons are more sought after.
* Other British toy train makers

of this era include: Bond's of Euston Road in London and Barr Knight of Glasgow in Scotland.

America
After World War I, the Lionel Corporation, with its larger, standard gauge of 57mm (compared to 35mm for '0' Gauge' and 48 mm for Gauge I), forced Ives to lose its previous advantage.
Marketing a range of colourful '0' Gauge and Standard Gauge products, Lionel dominated the market, even during the Depression of the 1930s.
* This solid 2-6-2 locomotive (below) is typical of the range produced. Other collectable locomotives include the 'City of Portland', a streamlined three-car set from 1934.
* American Flyer, Lionel's main rival, from 1934, also produced a popular range of trains.
* Ives were finally taken over by Lionel in 1928 and American Flyer by A.C. Gilbert in 1937.

'00' GAUGE
1922-1940

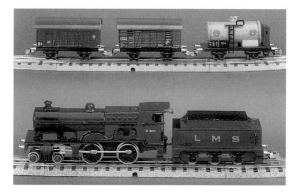

*A Märklin LMS E800 locomotive, tender and stock;
1938; '00' Gauge; value code B*

**Note: The range of trains produced is so vast and varied
it is impossible to give a single, definitive checklist.**

Table-top ranges

The tendency towards smaller
gauges after the end of World
War I led Bing to introduce a new
range of '00' Gauge table-top railway sets in 1922.

Followed later by other major
toymakers, the table-top principle was slightly adapted by each
one. Although generally modelled with a consistent track
width of ⅝in (16.5mm) between
rail centres, the proportion of
locomotive and rolling stock bodies tend to vary enormously
between different makers.

Initially made with clockwork
mechanisms, by the late 1920s
the number of sets available had
grown enormously to include an
electric version, as well as various
miniature tunnels, engine sheds,
stations and signal cabins.

Trix

After Bing's closure in 1933, Stefan
and Franz Bing, together with

Oppenheimer Erlanger, opened a
new toy company, naming it Trix.
They launched a novel constructor
set system, which was similar to a
smaller version by Meccano, but
pierced with many circular holes.
This was followed, in 1935, with a
German outline '00' Gauge electric train set, which proved an
immediate success, despite its
heavy, oversized wheels and unrealistic bodies.

The Trix table-top system had
several novel features, including:
* instant remote change of motor
polarity, enabling spectacular
sliding reverses,
* a three-rail system, enabling
realistic head-to-head running.

Bassett-Lowke

From 1935, Bassett-Lowke were
made the sole importer of Trix to
Britain, and when the Bing family moved to Britain for political
reasons, Bassett-Lowke helped to
develop the range.

One of the most celebrated locomotives produced was this 'Princess' Princess Royal class locomotive (bottom left) with a diecast body and tender:
* All Trix locomotive bodies and chassis were made of mazac, which was sturdy, but can crack and distort.
* The locomotives were sold in attractive presentation cases and a wide range of LMS (London Midland & Scottish) coaches were also available.

Rolling stock

These wagons (above) are made of lithographed tinplate and date from 1937.
* Pre-World War II models are distinguished by the diecast hook coupling and bent wire eye (often missing).

Southern stock

Trix modelled all the four major railway companies' stock, apart from those of the Great Western Railway. Their Southern Railway stock from this period is particularly sought after today and one of the rarest pieces they made is this boxed Southern Railway EMU (Electric Multiple Unit) set (below).
* It comprises a standard Trix motor squeezed into an under-sized bogie coach with a dummy trailer and centre coach.

Märklin

Märklin could not let the success of the Trix venture pass unchallenged. In 1935 they introduced their own '00' Gauge range, producing various German-outline stocks, locomotives and buildings.
* In good condition, the pieces have a highly lacquered jewel-like appearance.
* Fine detailing is characteristic of all these trains.
* Runs on a three-rail track, similar to Hornby-Dublo (which copied the Märklin design).
* Unfortunately many of the locomotives were made with diecast bodies, which often decay and crack.
* In general, export models are highly sought after.
* The 1938 LMS E800 by Märklin in the main picture is an extremely fine example of their work during this period.
* They crafted a special, finely detailed, miniature tinplate body for the locomotive and tender to resemble the LMS (London Midland & Scottish) Compound locomotive and tender.
* It is possible that fewer than 100 examples were ever sold in Britain, so making them highly sought after today.
* Distinguished from post-World War II examples by having black or silver spring claw couplings between the coaches.

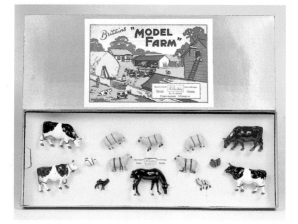

A Britains 'Model Farm' boxed set of toy lead figures, 1930s

Since Egyptian times miniature reproductions of military subjects have been made for children to play with as toys. But it was not until the mid 16thC that toy soldiers as we known them today were commercially produced. Lucotte and Mignot in France can be singled out as probably the first two recognised toy soldier manufacturers. Solid figures depicting the armies of France can be traced back to the 1760s. The German manufacturer, Georg Heyde also began to produce figures by the early 1800s.

Toy soldiers in these early days depicted the uniforms of troops or conflicts of the day. The overall dimension of a figure was about 2in (56mm), although in the case of German manufacturers this varied and usually resulted in a slightly smaller figure.

In the mid-19thC Continental manufacturers of toys had already taken the world lead in toy production and toy soldiers were no exception. In 1893, however, the situation changed drastically with the perfection of the hollow-cast method of manufacture devised in London by William Britain Junior, son of the founder of the Britains Company, which had previously been manufacturers of mechanical toys. This hollow-cast method revolutionised toy soldier production by way of its cost effective method of producing toys. The technique involves the pouring of a molten mixture of lead, tin and antimony into an engraved mould. As the antimony cools, it expands and gives fine detail to the casting without the support of solid metal.

British regiments were the first figures to be made by Britains using this process. Their success helped turn the British toy soldier market into a home-grown industry, eliminating Continental products which were expensive to import and sell. William Britain launched an advertising campaign based on a patriotic theme and his company has dominated the toy soldier scene even to this day.

As with any new successful venture, Britains had their competitors and it was not long before copies of Britains soldiers came on to the market. To combat this practice, each Britains mould was changed to incorporate the copyright presentation and the Britains name on the underside of the figure. Many successful prosecutions followed, and most of the firms responsible either stopped trading or designed their own unique range of figures.

John Hill & Co., founded by an ex-Britains employee became second to Britains in their scale of production. Hill was a successful rival of Britains throughout the period, up until World War II. The Continental manufacturers' challenge to the British toy soldier market having been defeated, the next hurdle was World War I. Production was severely disrupted but did not cease. A marked deterioration in the desire to accumulate war-like toys started to develop, and although the Britains ranges and those of their competitors were regularly updated, with the introduction of artillery, foreign troops and horse-drawn vehicles, military toy sales declined.

During the early 1920s Britains came up with the idea of non-military lead figures, resulting in the Home Farm Range (in the main picture). Although military sets still played a large part in Britains production, this, more peaceful subject resulted in increased sales both from those who had taken a dislike to war-like toys and, perhaps for the first time, the female child's desire to play with attractive figures. Farm carts, animals, shepherds and farm workers were followed by zoo animals in the early 1930s. Other non-military figures included footballers, boy scouts and figures from the Salavation Army.

Other manufacturers too had their own distinct ranges of figures. Taylor & Barrett enhanced their zoo figures with elephant rides, while Pixyland brought out a range of cinema and comic characters, including Pip, Squeak and Wilfred and Felix the Cat.

Britains secured many new contracts during the 1930s, including the rights to produce figures depicting Disney characters, a deal which provided souvenir items to Madame Tussauds' waxworks in London and the highly successful Cadbury's Cocoa scheme,with 'Cococubs' lead animals deposited in the top of cocoa tins. On the Continent, solids were still produced in profusion by Heyde of Germany and Mignot in France, while a new type of toy soldier emerged: the composition figure, which was usually 2⅜in (60mm) high. Produced mainly by Elastolin and Lineol in Germany, these figures represented uniforms of the German and Italian armies and their allies up to World War II.

By 1939, lead toy production was winding down. The resources of toy companies in the United Kingdom were switched to providing munitions for the impending war and production in lead ceased for the following six years.

SOLID FIGURES
1800-1940

A Lucotte 'grande guard'; c.1800;
2 ½in (60mm) high; value code H

Identification checklist for Lucotte solid figures 1760-1825
1. Is the figure made of solid lead?
2. Does it have a plug in the head and a soldered weapon (see below)?
3. Is it marked on the top of the base with the letters, L.C. and an image of the French Imperial Bee?
4. Is the figure 2in (56mm) in height? (Figures are generally measured in mm rather than cm or in.)
5. Does the figure represent a Napoleonic soldier?

Lucotte (1760-1825)
The first recognised commercially produced toy soldiers and figures can be attributed to the French company, Lucotte. Previously only flat figures had been available, made in Germany and Austria, but

Lucotte successfully produced a range of fully rounded, three-dimensional figures made of solid lead, such as the 'grande guard' French soldier in the main picture. The wide stride of the soldier is typical of all Lucotte figures.

Technique

Lucotte cast the body and head of the figures individually and inserted the head into the body by using a plug on the underside of the head.

Individual weapons and accessories were soldered on later.
* Each figure was slightly over 2in (56mm), slightly taller than the 2in (54mm) size toy figures recognised as standard today.

C.B.G. Mignot (1825-1993)

C.B.G. Mignot took over the Lucotte name and production in 1825 and continued to make solid toy soldiers up until 1993. They made the figures using the same technique, but extended the

Lucotte range to include uniforms from many periods of French history and 'Ancient and Modern Armies of the World'.

The 'Homme de Corvée' (above) made in 1920 is dressed in fatigue duty uniform and can be commonly found today.

Georg Heyde (c.1845-1949)

Heyde of Dresden in Germany were the next company to make a mark on the commercial toy soldier market. In addition to making figures in the, now standard, 2in (54mm) size, Heyde produced a distinctive range of items in a smaller scale of 1¾in (45mm), with brass moulds. Although Heyde used the same solid-cast technique as Mignot and Lucotte, he was more inventive, producing variations of figures.
* Mounted figures could be removed from their horses and were secured by a plug which was put into the rider.

Best known are the large display sets or set pieces, such as this Arab oasis group (above). By not simply concentrating on soldiers in action and parade poses, Heyde greatly enhanced their figures' appeal to both boys and girls.

Decline

European solid-cast figures dominated the toy market throughout the 19thC, exporting to England and other countries in vast quantities. However, the perfection of hollow-cast figures by William Britain Junior in England in 1893 was to end that domination. Although solid-cast toy soldiers remained popular in Continental Europe, they could not withstand the competition. Georg Heyde continued to manufacture until just after World War II, when the factory was bombed by the Allies.

Collecting

As solid figures are more easily found in the countries of origin, collectors mainly come from France, Germany and Italy, while British collectors tend to prefer hollow casts.

BRITAINS FIGURES (I)

A Britains Guards officer and drummer; 1920;
2in (54mm) high; value code H

Identification checklist for Britains' soldiers 1893-1945
1. Is the figure made of lead?
2. Is it 2in (54mm) high (measuring from the top of the base to the forehead)?
3. Does the underside of the base have a paper identifying label marked 'William Britain Junior' ?
4. Is the underside embossed with a date (post-1900 only)?
5. Is the base marked 'Britains Ltd Made in England Copyright'?
6. Is the figure in a box bearing the Britains' name?
7. Does the figure have a small air hole in the head?

Britains and Hollow casting
Since 1845, the William Britain Company had successfully manufactured a range of lead mechanical toys. A major development occurred in 1893, when William Britain Junior, son of the founder, revolutionised the toy industry by perfecting a method of manufacture which was to become known as hollow casting.

Technique
Moulds of iron and bronze were designed in two halves, hinged and attached to two wooden grips. Molten lead was poured into a bore hole in each mould, and the lead was then slushed around inside by the deft movement of the hand caster. The lead stuck to the sides of the mould and the excess was quickly poured back out into the melting pot, leaving the shell of the figure inside the mould. The air hole remained and was the route by which the excess was discarded. Rough edges were tumbled off and, finally, the figure was sent to be hand-painted.

This method enabled up to

four times as many figures to be made from a single quota of lead, equal to the amount it would take to make one solid figure. As a result, figures became less expensive to produce and the need for Britain to import toys greatly declined.

Soldiers

The first set of toy soldiers produced by Britains, in 1893, was of mounted Lifeguards. The venture was so successful that other British troops, both mounted and on foot, were quickly designed too.
* Foot soldiers all came in a standard size of (2in) 54mm, with mounted figures in a proportionately larger scale.

Guardsmen

Among the most important and collectable toy figures from this period are guardsmen, naval figures and the first khaki troops from the Boer War; vehicles were popular too.

This stretcher party, (above) is from the Royal Army Medical Corps. Made in 1908, the figures are part of a larger set, which included nurses and orderlies.

By 1900, William Britain had

produced over 100 different sets of toy lead figures.

Copies

Ironically, the success of Britains' figures led to a major problem for the company by the early 20thC. Many small firms, often managed by former Britains employees, opened factories, producing exact copies of Britains' early issues. Some of the more successful were Fry, Hanks, Davies and Mudie, all of whom were eventually prosecuted. These toys are extremely rare and sought after today.

Marks

One of the main reasons for this spate of copies was that Britains had never bothered to mark their lead figures.

In order to stamp out this major problem, Britains began to re-tool all their moulds in 1900, so as to incorporate the company name, date and the significant phrase 'Copyright of the Proprietors'. Re-tooling took several years and in the interim period small printed paper stickers were used on the underside of the base of each infantry figure.

Gamages

An important factor in Britains' success was a contract with Gamages, the famous department store in High Holborn, London. This stated that only Britains' soldiers would be featured in their toy department displays, thus giving them an important advantage over all their competitors in this field.

Collecting

Britains have the reputation as one of the finest makers of lead figures and so pieces are very sought after today. Early pieces, from the 1890s, are particularly desirable, as are figures and buildings from the revised range made by Britains between 1938 and 1941, just before war stopped toy production until 1945. These valuable charging Highlander and Piper pair from 1900 (left) have oval bases and originally had paper stickers on their bases too. As with many figures, the labels have fallen off over the years – always look for traces of glue on the base of the figures.

BRITAINS FIGURES (II)

World War I

Between 1914 and 1918 there were several new and important developments at Britains:

* Foreign troops and artillery were added to Britains' range, reflecting the current international conflicts in the uniforms worn by the toy soldiers and by the characteristic weaponry.

* More attention was given to packaging Britains' products, with the introduction of good-quality red cardboard boxes.

Civilian figures

To complement their military range, Britains produced a wide selection of civilian figures. These tended to be produced in sets with a particular theme, such as the Salvation Army.

A particularly popular set was the 'Famous Football Teams' range, comprising teams of footballers from all the major sides. This boxed set (in the main picture) made in 1920 comprises all the different players of the Aston Villa football team.

* Football teams were made for all major British clubs and some, now rare, overseas ones too.

Farms series

In the pro-disarmament mood of the 1920s, Britain saw a decline in the sales of military figures.

As an attempt to find a more peaceful alternative, Britains introduced the 'Home Farm' series, which was an immediate success and revitalised the toy figure market.

There was a large selection of figures to collect, from large pieces, such as the farm wagon and driver (below), to smaller, individual pieces, such as a shepherd and sheep.

Other characters included a farmer, two versions of the farmer's wife, as well as a range of farm animals.

One of the most sought after characters in the farm series is the village idiot.

It was not originally going to be part of the series, but was hurriedly designed and issued following a visit and comment made by Queen Mary at the 1927 British Industries Fair, when she was heard to remark that the Britains' farm set 'had everything but the village idiot'!

* The unusual history of the village idiot rather than its scarcity makes it an extremely sought after figure today with collectors.
* The village idiot figure was issued in a range of beige, pink, green and blue working smocks.

waxwork museum in London.

Perhaps the most successful of all these ventures was the commission obtained from the confectionery firm, Cadbury's, to supply 'Cococubs', small lead animals in human clothes (bottom) given away in tins of cocoa.

These toys were so popular that Britains found it necessary to open an additional factory in the north of England to cope with production! Today, they have remained highly collectable.

Zoo

The zoo was another successful series, featuring animals, cages and keepers.

This camel (below) was a standard zoo range issue and is not worth very much on its own, but is much more sought after when the rare sailor boy figure is added. (It is rare to see them together, as the boy is often separated.)

Licensing

During the 1930s Britains began to produce figures on behalf of other companies. This figure of Pluto (below) was produced for Walt Disney (see p.74) and the premium on any Disney memorabilia makes it a highly collectable figure.

Britains also made characters of Mickey Mouse, Snow White and the Seven Dwarfs.

Other figures include:
* Buck Rogers, the American space hero, who was made specially for an American breakfast cereal company.
* souvenirs for Madame Tussaud's

Other figures

Britains also made station staff and passengers for Bassett-Lowke, as well as '00' Gauge figures and accessories for Trix.

World War II

Production continued up until 1941, when all toy manufacturing stopped at Britains, in order for them to concentrate on producing munitions for the war effort.

OTHER HOLLOW-CAST FIGURES 1898-1940

A John Hill & Co. Highland officer with moveable sword arm; 1938;
2in (54mm) high; value code H

**Note: The range of hollow-cast figures is so vast and varied
that it is not possible to give a single, definitive checklist.**

Other makers
Britains' success with hollow-cast
figures encouraged many other
companies to copy their designs.
British firms such as Hanks, Fry
and Renvoize were all prosecuted for their pirate activities, but
they survived and went on to produce their own successful ranges of
original designs.

John Hill & Co. (1898-1959)
John Hill did not resort to copying, and produced a wide and
varied range of toy soldiers and
figures. The Highland officer in
the main picture is typical of their
pre-World War II figures and is in
sharp contrast to Britains' rigid
marching figures.
* Makers B.M.C. (Brushfield
Manufacturing Company) issued

many well-designed military
figures between 1900 and 1920,
such as this rare foreign service
troop (below).
* It is 2⅜in (60mm) in height.

Other British makers produced their own original figures and quickly became noted for particular categories of toy soldier or figures, thus enabling the market to stay healthy and competitive.

Charbens (1920-1955)

Initially, Charbens produced figures for other companies, but they soon developed their own unique line of mainly non-military figures. Their best known set of figures is the circus series made in 1935 which features this ringmaster and cyclists (below).

* Other figures from the circus included: acrobats, clowns, jugglers and animals, a comic policeman and even boxing midgets.

Taylor & Barrett (1920-1939)

The most famous hollow-cast set figures produced by the British firm Taylor & Barrett was a zoo series made 1920-1939.

More imaginative in design than Britains' version (see p.103), Taylor & Barrett zoo features a chimps' tea party set, parrots on a stand, a llama, camel and elephant ride (below), as well as children and zoo keepers.
* Other series included a wide range of lead vehicles, such as several made for Skybirds.

Collecting

During the course of the interwar period is was becoming clear to manufacturers that non-military subjects were proving popular with the toy-buying public. Soldiers were therefore increasingly replaced by a wider range of subject matter, such as the ones mentioned here.

Today, although pre-World War II figures by Britains remain the most popular with collectors, there is growing interest in other companies, which produced such a diverse and appealing range of toy figures.

Pixyland & Co. (1922-1932)

Pixyland was most famous for their lead figures of popular contemporary cartoon characters, such as Tiger Tim and the Bruin Boys, based on characters from 'Rainbow', a British children's comic popular in the 1920s. Other characters by Pixyland include Pip, Squeak and Wilfred (below, left), from the *Daily Mirror* cartoon, and cinema characters such as Dismal Desmond and Felix the Cat (below, right).

Pixyland had not acquired the licensing rights to use the Felix name and were compelled to market the toy figure in boxes named 'Cinema Favourites'.
* This one was made in 1926.

A Manoil 'Happy Farm' figure of a lady watering flowers; 1930s; American; 3in (65mm); value code H

Note: The range of hollow-cast figures is so vast and varied that it is not possible to give a single, definitive checklist.

Elastolin and Lineol (1920-1941)
The most successful toy figure manufacturers in Germany were Elastolin and Lineol, both famous for their composition figures. Composition was a method of manufacture perfected in 1910 and used throughout the 1930s.

Technique
An all-embracing title, composition applies to any toy soldier and figure made of a plaster-like substance. 'Elastolin' was the name of Hausser's composition

range. As with Lineol, Elastolin figures were made of kaolin, sawdust and glue which was moulded, after being heated around a wire frame. After 1933 many of the companies' toys were based on the German army and political leaders, such as Hitler, Hess, and Goering. They were made from composition with porcelain heads and moveable arms capable of saluting. They were accompanied by a range of tinplate vehicles.
* Other subjects included zoo and farm animals, such as this peacock (left) and the perennially popular cowboys and Indians.
* Elastolin figures have an oval base, while Lineol's have a rectangular base.
* Lineol's factory in Dresden was destroyed by Allied bombing during World War II, leading to its closure. Elastolin continued after 1945, converting to plastic in the 1950s and finally closing in 1984.

America
During the 1920s and 1930s in the United States, two major manufacturers flourished above all the others. Barclay and Manoil

both produced hollow-cast or slush-cast (as they are known in America) toy soldiers and figures, which were manufactured in a 2½in (70mm) scale.

Dimestores

Based in New York, Barclay and Manoil supplied their figures to five and ten cents dimestores, including famous stores such as Mayberry's and F.W. Woolworth.

Popular subjects included figures from the US Military, the Air Force and Navy:
* Note the distinctive oval base and slush-cast air holes under each foot.
* The standard size of the Barclay figure is 2½in (70mm).
* Barclay also made artillery and intricate models complete with integral anti-aircraft weapons and powerful searchlights. which were also popular.

'Happy Farm'

Barclay and Manoil did not copy each others' figures, but covered the same subject areas, so they are compatible with each other. A popular theme with both companies was American social history, reflected in the Manoil Co. issue of the 'Happy Farm' series, with farm workers and animals. The series, which included the figure of a lady watering flowers (in the main picture) was issued throughout the 1930s and is an idealised portrayal of an American farming family.
* The Wild West was portrayed by the 'My Ranch' series by Manoil, which features cowboys and cowgirls at play instead of traditional fighting scenes.
* Another firm, Tommy Toys (1920-25) made figures from nursery rhyme and fairy tale series, including Humpty Dumpty, Old King Cole and Puss in Boots.

This figure of Little Miss Muffet (above) was made by Tommy Toys in 1935 and is highly collectable today, although it can be seen that it has has suffered some slight damage.

Grey Iron (1920-1939)

Cast iron had been a popular material for toys in America since the 1860s. However, Grey Iron were the only company to use cast iron to make toy soldiers and figures.

Although they were popular, the figures were not of such good quality. as contemporary hollow-cast lead figures.

This skipping girl (above) is from a series based on the American family, at home, on the farm and at the beach:
* The (2in) 54mm scale was adopted by Grey Iron, in common with other manufacturers.
* Grey Iron also produced soldiers and civilians.

Collecting

American toys are rarely found in Europe, but they are worth looking out for as their value has risen considerably in recent years.

A Dinky Toys American export No.1 Commercial Vehicles Gift Set, c.1946-1948

The history of miniature vehicles dates back to the Edwardian period, when they were made as 'Penny Toys' (see p.44), modelled in lithographed tinplate and small enough to fit into a child's pocket. These types of toys were also produced in slush-cast lead versions in both Europe and America. Slush-casting is the crudest form of lead casting, with molten metal poured around an open mould. Although simply made, these small cars are very appealing and sought after today.

Also during the Edwardian period, William Britain first produced a wide range of horse-drawn vehicles, using the more sophisticated hollow-cast technique (see p.100). The earliest diecast models were small in size, about 2in (5cm) long, increasing to a standard 3in (7.5cm) by 1918.

After World War I, casting techniques improved, with better-quality models made by firms such as John Hill in Britain and Tootsie Toys in America. Tootsie Toys dominated the American market in diecast toys, with a vast range of products, such as aeroplanes and cars, as well as cooking stoves and dolls' houses.

Tootise Toys were also responsible for innovations in production technique. They were the first company to replace lead with mazac (a magnesium and zinc-based alloy) which was lighter and harder.

In 1931 the British toymaker Frank Hornby introduced a range of lead figures to accompany their Hornby Series railway layouts. They were initially called 'Modelled Miniatures' and included station figures and road vehicles and were an immediate success. By 1934 they had changed their name to Dinky Toys and became one of the most popular ranges of toys ever produced in Britain.

Dinky remained the world leader in diecast toys until the 1960s. In spite of interruption by World War II, they managed to maintain their standards during the 1940s and 1950s, adapting to change and adding new features and ranges to ensure continued popularity. In 1947 they introduced the Supertoy range, pieces from which which were larger and had more detailed features.

They also produced a range of light commercial vans, racing cars, sports cars, military vehicles and aircraft. Their 'Golden Age' is generally considered to be between 1958 and 1964, when they introduced different paint variations and attractive new issues.

Dinky was not without competitors, particularly in the years following World War II. One of their main rivals were Corgi, particularly between 1956 and 1968. Corgi were founded by Philip Ullman, head of Tippco, the successful German company, and he moved to Britain in 1933. Corgi Toys were of a very high standard and were sold in attractively designed boxes. A major selling point was the exciting features added to the toys.

Other important makers include Lesney and Spot-On. Lesney were founded in 1947 by two ex-servicemen. They produced an extremely successful range of diecast vehicles, the most innovative of which was the 'Matchbox' range, inspired by the idea of creating simple and affordable toys. The toys were sold in a box styled as a matchbox; the range was created in 1953 and is still in production today. Spot-On, another British company, also found success with their diecast vehicles. Their vehicles were slightly larger than Dinky Toys, well-modelled and, as with Corgi, packed with exciting and original features.

Diecast toys saw a decline in quality by the late 1960s. By 1970 the Dinky Toy range looked outdated compared with the more exciting Corgi range and in 1971, Triang, the holding company, went into receivership. Diecast toys continue to be produced in the Far East to the present day, but they are generally not of such a high standard.

DINKY TOYS & OTHER
MAKERS 1920-1940 (I)

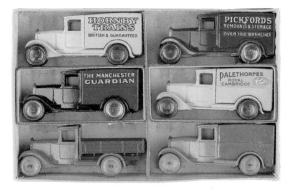

A Dinky Toy part set of four 28/1 series delivery vans in original trade box; 1934; value code B

Identification checklist for pre-World War II Dinky Toys
1. Is the vehicle made of soft lead (denotes it was made pre-1934)?
2. Does it have the correct marking on the underside?
3. Is the paint original?
4. Are the transfers original?
5. Are the front wings intact and the axles straight?
6. Are the windscreen pillars or clip holding the box section original?
7. Is the cab open (without windows)?

Early diecasts
In an attempt to revitalise the toy industry after the end of World War I, in 1918, the American firm, Tootsie Toys (1906-present) introduced a new range of innovative pocket-sized diecast toys, often depicting contemporary comic characters.

Britain was initially slow to develop these new pocket-sized and inexpensive toys after the end of World War I. Companies such as John Hill & Co., which were already well-known for toy figures, produced vehicles, but only in crude slush-cast lead and based on American designs.

* Other early makers including Taylor & Barrett (1920-1940) which also produced models, often complete with extra details, such as this Turntable Fire Escape (left) made c.1938, with a working ladder and separate cast crew members – a driver and a look-out man.
* It is not so detailed as early American diecast toys.

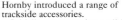

Modelled Miniatures

Tootsie Toys' success in America inspired Frank Hornby, one of Britain's leading toy manufacturers of this century, to try to do the same in Britain. Already a household name with his pre-war invention, 'Mechanics Made Easy' sets, later and more commonly known as Meccano (see p.68), in 1920 Hornby had decided to turn his attention to developing a new '0' Gauge toy railway system.

From 1924 onwards, to complement this railway system, Hornby introduced a range of trackside accessories.

Initially concentrating on lithographed tinplate suitcases, platform machines and milk churns, he then proceeded to make lead figures to accompany them. In 1931 the first figures were introduced as part of the 'Modelled Miniatures Series'.

Amongst the earliest issues were two white-coated painters, each with different coloured caps, carrying a board advertisement for 'Hall's Distemper', a type of household paint.

*It is still possible to find these figures today, but beware of reproductions, with figures carrying either a ladder or a recently-made advertising board.

Further issues included passengers and station and engineering staff, such as these 'No. 1 Series Station Staff' (left), which were made by Hornby in 1932.

Dinky Toys

The next step for Hornby was to add a range of pocket-sized vehicles, the first of which appeared in 1933. The set of delivery vans in the main picture neatly illustrates the development of these toys from 'Modelled Miniatures' to Dinky Toys.

The 22 Series motor truck and delivery van (at the bottom of the main picture) were issued as part of the Hornby Series, in 1933, while the four others, marked 'Dinky Toys' on the bases, are part of Dinky's first 28 Series.

* The name is believed to have been thought of by a young friend of one of Frank Hornby's daughters and is probably derived as a diminutive of the Scottish word, dink, meaning neat or fine.

Dinky did not just produce vans and motor cars. This colourful tractor (left) and the military tank (above) were part of the 22 series too and are also sought after by collectors.

Collecting

Early lead toys tend to be rare, and are therefore highly desirable. European collectors prefer Dinky Toys to American Tootsie Toys, but there is a large market for Tootsie Toys and other diecast toys in the United States.

Although initially marketed by Hornby as 'Modelled Miniatures', they became known as Dinky Toys in April 1934 and were an immediate success.

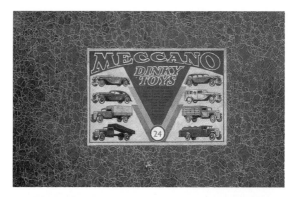

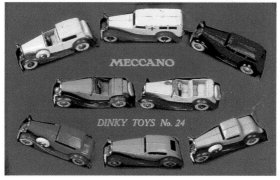

Diecast technique

In 1934 the use of lead was discontinued by Dinky Toys and replaced with injection-moulded diecast mazac (a magnesium and zinc alloy), copying the methods used by Tootsie Toys.

The 24 Series set of diecast saloon cars in the main picture highlights the typical features found in early Dinky Toys, such as stylish contemporary design and attractive colours. However, they also had weak points.

A properly produced diecast mazac toy should be indestructible, but, as Dinky discovered, if any impurities, such as lead, enter the alloy mix and there are undue stresses in the mould, fatigue will result. This causes the toys to expand, distort out of shape, crack or simply collapse into many smal pieces.

* Even in this rare and extremely valuable set, there are a few small signs of fatigue.

Vans

This group of 28 and 280 Series vans (opposite top) includes the second issue van from 1934, with shield-shape radiator and narrow door and the revised third type van, with a larger door and an eggbox grille, 1940-1941.
* The rare 'Bentalls' Van (below) currently holds the world record auction price for a Dinky Toy.

Originally produced as a promotional issue for the Kingston-upon-Thames department store, it is believed to be the only one to have survived.
* The 280 series continued in plain coloured variations after World War II, which are of small value and these sometimes found with fake transfers.

Variants
Between 1934 and 1940, Dinky Toys produced a wide range of miniature vehicles in several different series.

Confusingly, the series was not produced in any logical order, with some of the other most collectable ones including:
* 23 series racing cars
* 25 series lorries
* 30 series saloon and sports cars
* 36 series saloon and sports cars

* 38 series British sports cars
* 39 series American cars.

The group of 23 series racing cars (below) is a good illustration of how Dinky would often introduce many variations.
* The original issue was produced in April 1934 were available in red and yellow.
* This was followed by an interim casting variant in late 1934. Dinky also produced a rare blue and white 'humbug' variant, designed to replicate the actual record-breaking 'Magic Midget' driven by Captain George Eyston in 1933 and 1934.

Post-war variants
Almost all these models were produced again, after the end of World War II. Although they are superficially similar, they are usually very different in terms of rarity and detailed appearance:
* Pre-war models have thin axles, smooth, unridged hubs, are usually finished in primary colours and will have probably suffered from metal fatigue.
* Early post-war vehicles have thicker axles, ridged hubs and are usually finished in drab colours.

Condition
The tendency to distort and crumble is obviously of concern to collectors, and it is known that the Meccano Marketing department were receiving complaints in the 1930s about defective stock. But, fortunately, fatigue need not deter collectors interested in this field as, if kept in stable, moderate temperatures and away from direct, strong light and handled carefully, they should last indefinitely.

Collecting
One of the main reasons for the universal popularity of Dinky Toys is that, as their history is so well documented, it is nearly always possible to trace the history of each variation of these toys through contemporary retailers' catalogues and Meccano magazines or books on the subject.

DINKY TOYS 1945-1958

A Dinky Toys two-tone 39 series Oldsmobile 6 Sedan for the American market; c.1950-1952; 4in (10cm) long; value code E

Identification checklist for Dinky Toys 1945-1958
1. Does the car have thick axles and ridged wheel hubs?
2. Is the paint in original deep and lustrous finish?
3. Are the wheel hubs in a contrasting colour to the bodywork?
4. Is the car in a drab, single colour?
5. Are the tyres of the original type or period (see below)?
6. Is the baseplate in original unaltered condition?

Post-war Dinky Toys
With no new toys available since 1941, there was huge pent-up demand for new toys after the end of World War II. For Meccano, as with other companies, the transition from war production to renewed toy production did not take place quickly.

Under pressure to restart production, Dinky had no choice but to reissue many of their pre-war range, this time using thicker axles, a purer form of mazac (which rarely suffers from fatigue) and new (much duller) colours. The changes took time to implement, however, and issues made in 1946, such as the earlier verion of the Sedan in the main picture, still had certain pre-war features, such as smooth wheel hubs, white tyres and details such as silver highlighted side lights and door handles.

Various series
The most commonly found series between 1946 and 1952 are:
* 23 series racing cars, 25 series lorries, 30 series saloons, 38 series sports cars and the 39 series American cars.

Each series had minor detail variations and was slightly upgraded during the years of production. The Oldsmobile car was produced between 1946 and 1950 for the British market, but the one in the main picture is a special, and more collectable, hand-applied two-tone version made specially for the American market between 1950 and 1952.

Supertoys
In 1947 Dinky introduced the new Supertoy range – a fresh concept, which remained unrivalled by other manufacturers throughout this period. Their noticeable

feature was their large size. The No. 501 Foden diesel 8-wheel wagon (above), the first model made, was 3½ in (8.8cm) longer than the Oldsmobile Sedan.

Guy series
The companion commercial models in the Supertoy range were the Guy series of lorries, also first produced in 1947. Initially, the series comprised a range of lorries with similar body styles and was sold in utility brown boxes with plain labels. In 1949, Dinky added some of their most popular models to the Guy range. In emulation of the pre-war 28 series, one of the key features were advertising transfers on the sides of the vans.

The first model issued, and one of the most frequently found today, is the Slumberland van (below); therefore, condition of both vehicle and transfers are crucial to the value of the piece. Over the next

eight years new models were introduced, including vans advertising Spratts, Lyons Swiss Rolls, Ever Ready and Weetabix, the rarest, as it was produced only between 1952 and 1953.

Saloon cars
Dinky also introduced the 40 series of contemporary saloon cars, featuring the Riley Saloon, in 1947, and the Hillman Minx, Morris Oxford, Austin Taxi and the Austin Somerset by 1954.

Well-detailed replicas, they are of particular interest when found in unusual colour variations, such as the blue Morris Oxford Saloon (above). Each model had a typical colour range, such as grey, black, pale blue, green and red, and it is likely that rarities were created when the production quota had to be fulfilled and one particular paint spray had run out, so another was used in small quantities to make up the batch.

Other ranges
Dinky also produced a range of light commercials, racing cars, sports cars, military vehicles and aircraft. Military vehicles, comprising mainly pre-war reissued models during the late 1940s and early 1950s, were relaunched in 1953 with a wide range of vehicles from the recently re-equipped British Army.

This Avro Vulcan delta wing bomber is one of the rarest aircraft produced by Dinky. Owing to its colossal wingspan 6⅛in (15.6cm), it was difficult to maintain a high casting quality and

production was short-lived, so it is highly sought-after today.
* Other more commonly found aircraft include Tempest II fighter planes and the Viking airliner.

*A Dinky black and cream 161 Austin Somerset saloon in original box;
1956; 3½in (9cm); value code G*

**Note: The range of Dinky Toys is so varied, that it is not
possible to provide a single, definitive checklist.**

Developments

As prosperity returned to Britain
in the mid-1950s, Meccano
Limited saw the opportunity to
upgrade their best-selling ranges,
particularly Dinky Toys and
Hornby-Dublo trains.

The first signs of this new look
appeared in 1956 with the use of
different paint variations to
enhance ageing models. The car
in the main picture is a rare black
and cream version of the Austin
Somerset saloon, originally introduced in 1954, but part of a range
that was outdated in appearance.
* With two-tone variants and the
cheerful paint schemes also used
on the two Jaguar XK120s (below),
Dinky at this time put back some
of the vibrant colours which had
been missing from all their products since before the start of
World War II.

Commercial vehicles

The Dinky Toy commercial
vehicle range was revised during
this period. In 1959 a series of
BBC Television vehicles was
introduced, with an even rarer
series of ABC Television vehicles derived from the same castings introduced in 1962.

The ABC Television Outside Control Room (left, centre) reflects Dinky's attention to detail. Note the striking coloured box and how the camera and cameraman are linked to the van with cables.

Although well-established as successful toymakers by 1960, Dinky Toy production was still occasionally erratic, with uneconomic product runs involving expensive set-up costs. One of the most famous examples was the rare 920 Guy Warrior Heinz van from 1960, found with and

without plastic windows. It is probable that fewer than 1,000 such vans were ever produced.
* It combines a Guy Warrior chassis and box van from the earlier Guy Otter lorry.
* This van must not be confused with the larger 'Big Bedford' Heinz van (above), which is far more common, and made from a different casting.
* Different transfers can greatly affect a van's value. 'Big Bedford' vans advertising tomato ketchup are far more valuable than those which have a Heinz baked beans advertising transfer.

Buses
Of the many entirely new castings used during this period, some of the most successful were buses. The Dinky AEC or Leyland-type double decker buses had remained fairly similar in appearance since they were first introduced in 1938.
* In 1962, a new model was introduced – the revolutionary rear-engined Leyland Atlantean Bus, which had a front entrance with concertina doors.

Gift Sets
Gift sets were introduced towards the end of this period in a fresh style of display box with a special folding lid.

The cars in this top-of-the-range Mayfair set (bottom) were taken from current lines, with some models painted in unusual colours and with plastic figures.

Takeover
The huge cost of re-tooling and marketing their diverse new range of products had resulted in prohibitively expensive toys and trains. Facing a liquidity crisis, the board of Meccano Ltd., the parent company, agreed to a takeover in 1964 by Triang, their main rival. Although Dinky Toys survived for another 15 years, the takeover marked the end of the Golden Age.

France
Dinky's factory in France produced its own range of French cars, commercial vehicles and aircraft during this period and continued to do so right through the 1960s, even when Dinky in England had declined.

*A 261 Corgi Toy James Bond's Aston Martin DB5 from the film,
'Goldfinger'; 1965; 8in (20cm) long; value code H*

Identification checklist for Corgi Toys 1956-1968

1. Does the toy have a diecast body?
2. Are the wheels spoked?
3. Is 'Corgi Toys' cast into the base?
4. Does the toy still have its original box, accessories, inserts and instructions?
5. Is the packaging of good quality?
6. Is the toy designed with interesting and attractive features and details?
7. Does the toy contain several ingenious devices?

Mettoy (1936-83)

As with many great British companies, the origins of Corgi lie overseas. In 1933 Philip Ullman, head of Tippco, a very successful German toy company, moved to Britain. Initially, he worked as a subcontractor to other toymakers. In 1936, however, he decided to set up his own company, Mettoy, in Northampton and created a range of lithographed tinplate cars, aircraft and other road vehicles.

It has sometimes been assumed that Ullman brought his own dies for these toys from Germany as they are similar to those used for Tippco toys, but they were made in Britain, copying his own designs.

In 1946 the company started to expand, producing a limited range of large-scale diecast models. In 1948, as production boomed, Mettoy built a 14-acre factory near Swansea in Wales which remained a toymaking centre for the next 40 years.
* A new range of slightly smaller diecast models under the brand name, Castoys, were manufactured here from early 1950s onwards, but these were superseded in 1956 with a new series of toys.

FORD CONSUL SALOON

Corgi Toys

Spurred on by Dinky's success, Mettoy decided to create a range of diecast toys at the new factory in Swansea, with the corgi, a hardy Welsh dog, as an appropriate brand image. The toolmakers required to make the new dies were imported from Germany and the resulting toys were of a very high standard. This Ford Consul (above) is one of the first vehicles produced by Corgi and came complete with an attractively designed box.
* Note the plastic windows – unlike Dinky Toys at this time, whose cars were always produced with open windows, Corgi cars were all fitted with plastic ones.

Features

Keen to maintain its position as a brand leader in producing value-for-money feature-packed toy vehicles in a small body shell, in 1959 Corgi added spring suspension to vehicles and in 1963 produced a Ghia-bodied Chrysler V8, with opening doors, folding seats, an opening bonnet and a corgi on the back parcel shelf.

However, one of Corgi's best, and most famous, toys, was the James Bond's Aston Martin, in the main picture.

Corgi used their existing Aston Martin DB4, first produced in 1964, as the basis for the model and tried to pack in as many features and devices as possible to emulate those in the Aston Martin DB5 used in the 1964 James Bond film, 'Goldfinger'.

Among the main features were:
* a front machine gun
* rear bullet-proof shield
* an operating ejector seat.

Corgi engineers devised a special test rig to operate the ejector seat to ensure that it would function faultlessly. Their test was a success and the toy was launched in November 1965 and was acclaimed as the 'Toy of the Year' by the National Association of Toy Retailers.

In its original three-year production run, the James Bond Aston Martin became one of the most popular toys ever made, with nearly three million sold.
* Although the car is illustrated in silver on the packaging, the toy was initially painted gold – in order to underline its 'premium quality' status.
* The rarest version of the James Bond Aston Martin is a revised 1968 model which was slightly larger and painted in silver. It also had extra features: rotating number plates and even telescopic tyre slashers.
* It is worth three times as much as the gold version.

Rally cars

Among the more popular series produced by Corgi was a range of rally cars current between 1964 and 1970. Enthusiasm for rallies in Britain had begun with successes in actual races, particularly Paddy Hopkirk's triumphant win in the Monte Carlo Rally in 1964 in a Mini Cooper. Note that:
* Corgi produced rally versions of existing toy vehicles by adding on extra lamps, transfers and roof racks.
* Cars were regularly updated and Corgi chronicled all the major rallies until the Hillman Hunter World Cup rally car of 1970.

This 1965 Monte Carlo rally set (below) comprises a rare group of vehicles, which, remarkably, are still in pristine condition. However, the overall appeal is let down by the poor quality of the artwork on the packaging.

LESNEY & SPOT-ON

A Lesney Toys Prime Mover Set; 1950;
12in (30cm) long; value code F

Note: The range of toys is so vast and varied that it is not possible to provide a single, definitive checklist.

Lesney Toys

Lesney Products were founded in 1947 by two old school friends, Leslie Smith and Rodney Smith, who had both recently been discharged from the Navy.
* The company name was invented by combining their Christian names and they established their premises in an old pub in Edmonton, north London.

Having already gained some experience in toymaking before World War II – Rodney had worked for DCMT (see p.124) – in 1948 Lesney introduced a range of diecast toys. One of the first issues was a 4in (10cm) long Crawler Tractor, which, by 1950, had developed into a Bulldozer as part of the Prime Mover Set in the main picture.

From 1950 onwards, Lesney's products were exclusively retailed by the long-established

Anglo-German firm, Moses Kohnstam Ltd., whose name 'Moko' appears beside Lesney on their toys until the late 1950s.
* It is worth noting though that not all Moko toys c.1950 were made by Lesney.

Models of Yesteryear

Models of Yesteryear were first introduced in 1956 and are still in production today (although in a different form and produced in China). The series was immensely popular from the start.

Adults started to collect these toys too and now it is rarer to see them unboxed than boxed.
* The early 1960s represented the peak of quality and collectability. Apart from odd wheel and colour variations, the later 1960s Matchbox and Yesteryear models tended to be more garish and are less popular today.

Matchbox

In 1953 Jack Odell, co-founder of Lesney, created their most famous range, Matchbox Toys, inspired by the idea of creating simple and easily affordable toys for children.

A typical example is the 1958 Commer Pick-Up (right) – the commercial version of the Hillman Minx – in original form with metal wheels and a plain 'Moko' box.
* In 1962 Lesney made a two-colour version, with black plastic wheels and a more elaborate box – worth five times as much, as

few were made, even though overall production was then running at a total of one million models a week!

Typical features
Spot-On toys came with fully fitted interiors and windows and 'Flexomatic' suspension – probably the most accurate model suspension of any diecast. Electric head lamps were also added between 1961 and 1962.
* They also came in a rich variety of colours giving scope for collecting variations of each model.
   Almost any complete boxed set is rare – the boxes are fragile and easily damaged – and so are highly valued.
* Nevertheless, Spot-On prices have moved little in the past 10 years, so they still represent a good area within the diecast field to start collecting.

* Overall, Matchbox toys have constantly increased in value over the past 10 years, while the value of Models of Yesteryear has remained static.

Decline
In 1969 the American toymakers, Mattel, introduced their cheaply made 'Hot Wheels' range, designed with low-friction axles to run down special plastic tracks. As turnover slumped as a result of this competition, Lesney were forced to retool and produce a newly adapted 'Superfast' range. Garish in colour and of poor quality, these models are still not popular today.

Spot-On
Spot-On diecast toys were started by Lines Brothers in 1959. Modelled to 1/42 scale, they were slightly larger than Dinky Toys at 1/43, and were packed with features.

Scale
The reduction of a vehicle to a model scale is a complicated technique to perfect and proportions often have to change to allow for the differing viewpoint. Whereas Dinky Toys can look too 'thin' and Corgi Toys too 'fat', Spot-On achieved a successful sculptural roundness in their vehicles, setting them apart from other makers.

Buses
Spot-On's most famous model is probably the London Transport 'Routemaster' bus, introduced in 1963 (above). Apart from using stock wheels, it is a very accurate representation.

Haulage vehicles
In 1960, Spot-On introduced a range of heavy trucks, but because of high overheads, this series sadly ended in 1963.

Decline
From February 1964, Lines Brothers took over Meccano (including Dinky Toys), so the need to produce the more expensive Spot-On toys diminished. In 1967 the factory at Castlereagh in Northern Ireland closed, and production finally ceased.

One of the last – and rarest – diecast models ever produced by Spot-On was the hugely popular Batmobile from the 'Magicar' series (left). This toy used the small, but powerful, Wrenn Maximiser electric motor.

DINKY & CORGI TOYS'
DECLINE 1964-1979

A Dinky 'Thunderbirds 2' space craft; c.1967;
10in (25cm) long; value code A

Note: The range of toys is so vast that is is not possible to provide a single, definitive checklist.

Dinky Toys 1964-1971
Dinky continued to flourish for several years under the control of Triang by implementing some important changes. Most significantly, they tried to rationalise the production of simpler saloon models by designing new cars, which were less expensive to produce and were packed with features and even experimented with production in Hong Kong. They also made other changes:
* Between 1965 and 1966 they experimented with cellophane and card packaging. Although this was meant to enhance the appearance of the product, the boxes were fragile and were easily damaged. Therefore, from 1967 onwards, they were replaced by practical, although less attractive, hard plastic cases.
* Until the late 1960s, Corgi's success in negotiating the manufacture of licensed products from television or film programmes had been almost unchallenged. However, in 1967, Dinky did succeed in winning the contract to produce two different models from Gerry Anderson's highly

successful Thunderbirds children's television series.
  Unlike the lightweight plastic models of other TV21 products made by Lincoln Inc. in America and Rosenthal in Hong Kong, the Dinky Thunderbird 2 in the main picture and Lady Penelope's FAB 1 (below) were solid and well-detailed models.
* As was often the case, the first issues of these models are the most interesting and valuable.
* The first Thunderbird 2 was finished in pale green, replaced by metallic blue/green from 1973 and worth considerably less.

* All versions of Thunderbird 2 feature spring-operated extending legs and a detachable pod with a small Thunderbird 4 contained inside.
* Lady Penelope's FAB 1 has a sliding canopy with a large missile firing from behind a radiator grille and rear-firing harpoons.
* Although well-produced, the card packaging on these toys is fragile and it is hard to find them in good condition today.

Other novelty tie-ins included Stripey the Magic Mini (below), also produced in 1967 and based on a Gerry Anderson comic strip.

STRIPEY - the Magic Mini 107

However, the concept of banana yellow pandas driving a Mini did not catch on with children and neither the comic or model were successful – nor are they very collectable today.

'Speedwheels'
This vehicle (right) is a Dinky Toy Ford Capri, produced in 1969 and featuring the latest 'Speedwheels'. In common with Corgi and Matchbox, Dinky were forced to rush through this new feature after Mattel introduced 'Hotwheels' in 1968. Although the wheels were inexpensive and poorly-made, the cars came with a section of racing track and greatly appealed to all children.
* Speedwheels were not such successful features on larger cars

as the detailing was weak and the axles bent easily, making the toys instantly unusable.

Closure
In general, the balance of the Dinky Toy range looked outdated by 1969-70 compared to the more vigorous Corgi models. In 1971 the Triang holding company went into receivership, brought down by competition, the diversity of their product range and the constant assault from cheaper overseas manufacturers, particularly those based in the Far East.

Corgi Toys
Between 1968 and 1970, the decline in standard at Corgi was far less noticeable than at Dinky, as they were still buoyed up by the success of film and TV-related models (such as James Bond cars and The Avengers gift set).

After the novel features of the 'Golden Jacks' models in 1969, with removable wheels on a number of models in 1970 Corgi introduced their 'Whizzwheels' range to compete with Mattel's 'Hot Wheels' series.

They achieved this by replacing cast-hubs and rubber tyres with grotesque single-piece plastic castings and thin axles. The series was made from a revived range of vehicles in garish colours, mostly based on old diecast models.

DINKY TOYS 165   FORD CAPRI

Commerical vehicles
Dinky's commercial vehicles saw a dramatic decline in quality too during the 1960s. Some of the best-known vehicles from this period include the popular AEC

Hoynor Car Transporter, the AEC BRS delivery service lorry, the AEC petrol tanker and the highly successful 905 Leyland dumper truck (left), produced by Dinky in 1966.

Although the Transporter was launched as a new toy, the modellers had simply altered the 936 Leyland chassis to accomodate the more up-to-date tilt cab and a tipping body.

OTHER BRITISH DIECASTS 1945-1970

A Shackleton Toys tipper lorry; 1950;
12½in (32cm) long; value code F

Identification checklist for Shackleton Toys 1948-1952

1. Are the parts intact?
2. Is the toy brightly coloured?
3. Does the toy still have its original box?
4. Is it a tipper lorry?
5. Does it have a clockwork mechanism?
6. Are the wheel stub axles made of diecast metal?

British diecasts

Many small toy companies specialising in diecast toys flourished during the peak years of production in the 1940s and 1950s. Some makers, such as Charbens, Benbros and Barrett & Sons, were based in north London, while Shackleton Toys were based in Cheshire.

Shackleton Toys (1948-1952)

Shackleton produced a range of large-scale diecast Foden FG lorries. Their first issues were flat-bed lorries, with a Dyson trailer added in 1949 and the rarer Tipper Lorry (in the main picture) added in 1950.
* Bear in mind that these lorries were mainly built from large and sturdy diecastings, with a brass and steel clockwork motor. The diecast parts often suffer from fatigue, particularly the leaf springs in the suspension.
* Shackleton Toys were more

expensive than Dinky Toys, and lack of availability of materials during the Korean War in the early 1950s and low sales led to the company's closure in 1952.

Crescent Toys (1922-1981)

Until 1950, Crescent Toys successfully marketed a range of simple, but attractive, toys produced for them by the firm DCMT (Diecast Casting Machine Tools Ltd.) based in Palmer's Green in London.
* DCMT later became famous as Lone Star, producing a range of soldiers, Treble-O miniature diecast push-along and electric table-top railway, military vehicles and the 'Impy' series of Matchbox-size vehicles in the 1960s. Few are collectable now.

Crescent moved production to Wales in 1950 and made a varied range of diecast toys, including three semi-trailers, similar to real ones used by British Rail in box

van form, with Scammell Scarab three-wheel tractors and various military models. The most sought-after toys are 10 different Grand Prix racing cars made between 1956 and 1960.
* The modelling of these racing cars (above) is of such good quality that they are more valuable than the equivalent Dinky Toy 23/230 series.

Chad Valley (1823-present)
Already well-established as makers of a variety of toys and games before World War II, Chad Valley produced an enhanced range of lithographed tinplate and aluminium toys during the 1940s. They also made diecast toys, notably the Weekin range of clockwork toys for the Rootes Group (makers of Sunbeam and Hillman cars) and are best-known for their superb range of 1/6th scale tractors.

More model than toy in appearance, the 1952 Fordson Major (below) was the first tractor produced. Sold in a plain brown box, which belied the quality of

the toy inside, the tractor was powered by a clockwork motor wound using the starting handle.
* Tractors made in 1954 are more modern in appearance than the 1952 models, and come in two versions, with or without a clockwork motor. Rarest of all is the promotional model of the famous grey 1955 Ferguson tractor, made by Ford for the industrialist, Harry Ferguson.

Other makers
Toy wholesalers, Morris & Stone, based in north London, used the brand name, Morestone, and marketed their toys as Modern Products. Between 1954 and 1959 they also produced their own range of diecast toys, including models such as the popular series of Noddy vehicles, the Esso Petrol Pump series of cars (still very affordable today) and larger toys, such as this Bedford 'S'-Type Car Transporter, made c.1957 (below).
* Although much rarer than an equivalent one made by Corgi (see p.118), the Morestone version is less valuable today.

In 1959, Morris & Stone introduced the eclectic Budgie range of toy vehicles.

However, the company was never able to compete with the major makers head-on, and ended up concentrating on tourist shop demand for buses and taxis. One of its successor companies still survives today.

EUROPEAN & AMERICAN DIECAST TOYS

A Tootsie Toy 'Autogiro; 1930s;
6in (12.5cm) value code B

Note: The range of toys is so vast and varied that it is not possible to provide a single, definitive checklist.

Other diecast makers
Nearly every industrialised country in the world produced their own, home-grown diecast toys. The following is just a selection of the most interesting diecast toys that can still be easily found today and which are collectable.

Tootsie Toys (1906-present)
Having created the first diecast toys in 1906, Tootsie Toys produced their finest models in the early to mid-1930s, most notably their range of Graham and La Salle automobiles, as well as vehicles from other car manufacturers, such as Ford, Lincoln, De Soto and Auburn. The 'flying' Autogiro in the main picture made in the late 1930s is from a different casting from their 1934 version, and is much rarer.

After World War II models became more unrealistic and cruder in appearance, with poor detailing to lower bodies, axles and open bases. By the 1970s their toys were even simpler in design, and made of plastic.

Märklin
A company the size of Märklin could not ignore the success of Dinky and Tootsie Toys, and introduced their own diecast range in 1935. Their range was similar to the diecast toys produced by Dinky, covering racing cars, record cars, limousines, streamlined tourers as well as military vehicles:
* Many pre-war models are now extremely scarce and are very sought after today.
* Look for ones with boxes.

The 1957 model Mercedez-Benz 300 SL (right) is a good example of the crisp detail and excellent quality casting of Märklin's diecast production throughout the 1950s.

Apart from a stylish fastback 1949 Buick, post-World War II production concentrated on German vehicles, including popular models by Mercedes-Benz, Volkswagen and Porsche, and trucks by Krupp and Magirus.

The 1940s and 1950s are probably the optimum period to collect, as the range acquired more 'features' by the 1960s and lost its precisely cast appearance.
* The last new model appeared in 1971 and production finally ceased in 1977.

Italy

The finest period for Italian diecast manufacture was the 1960s, with manufacturers such as Mebetoys, Polistil and Mercury, producing a range of attractive and high-quality diecast vehicles.

Of these three manufacturers, Mercury's vehicles are notably better-detailed and have less heavy bases than Mebetoys and Polistil and are of much greater value today.

Other makers

Other unusual diecast toymakers to look out for include:
* Metosul from Portugal
* Gamda from Israel
* Lion Car from Holland
* Septoy Gasquy from Belgium

Tekno

Tekno, a Danish company, manufactured a range of tinplate fire engines, ambulances and aircraft before and just after the end of World War II. They began by producing a range of crude, but appealing, Ford and Buick lorries in the late 1940s, and by the 1960s had developed a range of cars and lorries, packed with appealing features.
* One of their finest and most collectable diecast toys is the Mercedes-Benz 230SL (left), which has narrow door shut-lines and fingertip steering action.
* Commercial vehicles in unusual liveries are particularly sought after.

France

Founded in 1932, Solido are the most famous of all the French diecast companies, producing a range of diecast vehicles and cannon construction sets before World War II. (These are now rare and prone to fatigue.)

Today, the company is mainly known for their successful military vehicle range, which they started in 1961.
* Other French makers include JRD, CIJ-Europarc and Norev, which produced various plastic models until 1971.

The 100 Series vehicles, launched in 1957, are very attractive, exemplified by this 1964 Aston Martin DB5 Vantage (left), of much better quality than the Corgi version.

DIECAST TOYS
1970-PRESENT

A Dinky Toys Citröen Presidentielle; c.1970; 8in (20cm) long
value code F

**The range of diecast toys is so vast and varied, that it is
not possible to provide a single definitive checklist.**

1970-present

By 1970, most major diecast toy-makers worldwide were suffering from competition, both from domestic and overseas rivals, with consequent pressure on margins resulting in a noticeable overall decline in quality.

Dinky Toys

In 1971 Lines Brothers went into receivership, and Dinky Toy production was taken over by Airfix, which were already well-known for their model construction kits. Airfix continued to produce current Dinky Toy models but only in garish colours. Poorly detailed toy cars were added and the range sold in fragile vacuformed packaging. In general, Dinky Toys from this period until the closure of their Binns Road factory in Liverpool in 1979 are much less collectable, even when they are in perfect condition.

Fortunately, Dinky's French factory at Bobigny continued independently, producing some of the finest diecasts ever made between 1969 and 1972, notably the range of GMC lorries and commercial sets.

The finest model of all is the Citröen Presidentielle – the one in the main picture is a special edition version complete with electric head lamps.

Unfortunately, production was transferred to the Pilen factory in Spain in 1977, and the French company finally closed down for good in 1981.

Lesney Toys

As the 'Superfast' range of Matchbox vehicles became increasingly more colourful and gimmicky, the Models of Yesteryear range became more popular with adult collectors. They were produced in cellophane-fronted boxes with a huge range of liveries on a few models, most are now worth little as the market is saturated.

The 1912 Ford Model T (opposite, bottom) is typical of the range of Models of Yesteryear produced by Lesney, with typical features including bright colours, transfers and garish plastic features.

In 1982, Lesney was taken over by Universal Holdings, a Hong Kong company, which, in 1992, sold the business to Tyco which are based in America.
* They are also owners of the Dinky Toy brand name and models are produced in China.

Other makers

In Europe, companies such as NZG and Siku in Germany still produce fine commercial vehicles and cars, as do companies such as Herpa, Bang, Schabak, Gama and Tekno (revived as a Dutch company specialising in truck models). In France, Solido was taken over by Majorette, and their celebrated military range still makes an interesting collecting area. However, their earlier vintage pieces, and those by Rio and Brumm, have not proved popular with collectors.

Quality models by Bburago and Polistil from Italy are still popular, but new Far Eastern makers, such as Maisto, better them in detail and price, so are possibly a better investment.
* In general, it seems likely that European manufacture will continue to wither, as the domination of Far Eastern production is supported by American capital.

Lledo and EFE

EFE (Exclusive First Editions) were established in 1989 to make a range of '00'/H0 scale commercial vehicles, such as this boxed plastic lorry (above) with 'Start-rite' advertising transfers on the side. Lledo was founded in 1982 and they produce a collectable and keenly priced range.

Corgi Toys

Although there was a general decline in quality, Corgi enjoyed a late flowering between 1970 and 1972, producing a range of highly collectable models during this period, such as Noddy Cars, the Popeye Paddle Wagon and the ever-popular Magic Roundabout series of vehicles and figures.
* Most Corgi products were made with plastic parts at this time.

More typical of Corgi production in this period is this 1978 Charlie's Angel's Custom Van, of much poorer quality than their previous products, and worth little more today than its original price.

In 1983, Mettoy, the Corgi holding company, went into receivership, continuing as a management buy-out. They were taken over by Mattel in 1992, and production switched to China.

JAPANESE TOYS
1945-1970

A Nomura tinplate Buick Roadmaster 'Electric Mobile', early 1950s

In 1939, at the start of World War II, Germany still dominated the world market for toys, as it had done since the mid 19thC. Close behind were Britain, France and America and trailing after them was Japan, known only for making cheap, poorly made copies of European designs. By the end of the war in 1945, the situation had altered dramatically. Nazi Germany had been defeated by the Allies and its economy lay in ruins. Many of its best-known toy companies had collapsed during the war, while those which had survived faced a hard financial future. In the Far East, however, a remarkable development was taking place.

As with Germany, Japan had been defeated by the Allies in 1945 and had to endure seven years of Allied control. Against all odds, Japan made a dramatic economic recovery and its toymaking industry quickly became the most important in the world for the next 20 years, successfully producing large numbers of well-made but inexpensive toys for an international market.

America was a key player in Japan's success from the start. Large American toy companies, such as Rosko and Cragstan, were quick to seize the opportunity of capitalizing on Japan's huge resources. Production and labour costs were lower in Japan than in the West, and, in spite of the enormous size of Japan's toy industry, its infrastructure was still unsophisticated. For example, a patent number is seldom seen on either toy or box, although some toys have 'Pat.Pend.' printed near the trademark, and little is known about the companies, except that they were generally small, family run and adept at responding to changes in the marketplace. Some of the main names to look out for during this period include Alps, Bandai, Taiyo, Ichiko, Masudaya, Marusan and Nomura.

Therefore, it was extremely profitable for American toy

companies such as Louis Marx to commission Japanese firms to make toys specifically for them.

As a result, many post-war Japanese toys reflect contemporary American culture and tastes. Popular subjects included police cars, fire engines, and US Air Force aeroplanes, and figures were based on typical American children, often with red hair and freckly faces, and dressed in dungarees or jeans and check shirts!

Among Japan's most important achievements during this period was its development of celluloid and plastic, first used in America in the 19thC, but largely ignored by Western toy-makers, who still preferred to use tinplate. The Japanese saw the potential of plastic as a cheap and safe material and from the early 1950s onwards used it in a wide range of toys.

Japan produced a wide variety of traditional toys, such as cars, motorcycles and clockwork trains during this period, but is best known for its many extremely original and innovative designs, most particularly robots and space toys. The 1950s and 1960s saw the start of the race into space, which began in earnest in October 1957 with the first Sputnik satellite orbiting Earth and culminating in 1969 with the landing of man on the moon. In response to these technological advances, and the subsequent craze for pulp science fiction, Japanese toymakers gave full rein to their creative talents, producing enormous numbers of tinplate robots and space toys.

Equally successful were Japanese novelty toys. Made from plastic, tinplate and fabric or a combination of all three, these toys, often based on well-known American television personalities, were also capable of complicated movements, such as smoking a pipe or shining shoes, and were as popular with adults as children.

Brightly coloured, with noisy and sometimes aggressive special effects, such as 'Rotate-O-Matic Super Astronaut', whose chest compartment opens and fires noisily, these battery-operated toys and robots marked a major step forward in toy design and were instantly popular. The use of battery-operated mechanisms allowed toys to perform much more complicated movements than clockwork and to run for longer periods – making them very attractive to children, although more expensive.

Generally, clockwork and friction-powered toys date from the 1940s and early 1950s and battery-operated toys from the 1950s and 1960s. When selecting a battery-operated toy remember to take a selection of different batteries with you, if you want to establish whether it is still in working order.

By the late 1960s, Japan began to lose its supremacy over the international toy market, as cheaper diecast models and juvenile plastic toys from countries such as China flooded the market. New safety regulations came into force restricting the use of dangerous and sharp tinplate, giving guidelines on the constituents of paint, increasing production costs and thus making it less economically viable for American companies to buy Japanese toys.

JAPANESE TINPLATE
1945-1970

*A Masudaya lithographed tinplate battery-operated motorcyclist; late 1950s;
12in (30.5cm) long; value code F*

**Identification checklist for Japanese tinplate toys
1945-1960s**
1. Is the toy battery-operated (batteries usually
inside toys)?
2. Is it marked?
3. Is it made of lithographed tinplate?
4. If it is a transport vehicle, does it have
operating lights?
5. Does the toy have a sophisticated working action?
6. Is it composed of several articulated parts joined
together with metal 'tabs'?
7. Does it have an On/Off switch?

Japanese tinplate
At the end of World War II, Japan
was quick to recover from her
economic problems to become an
major player in the international
toy market. The industry comprised many firms, making a wide
variety of tinplate toys.

Masudaya (founded 1924)
Masudaya was one of many successful firms flourishing in Japan
after 1945, mass-producing good-
quality, lithographed tinplate

toys. Supported by the US distributor, Cragstan of New York,
who commissioned large numbers
of toys, the Japanese were quick
to respond to Western children's
tastes. The motorcyclist in the
main picture was certainly
produced specifically for the
Western market, but notice
that, although the bike and the
box look American, the cyclist's
face is definitely Japanese!
Transport vehicles, particularly
motorbikes, were popular

subjects. This one by Marusan (below) was made between 1960 and 1965 and is based on a real model of a popular Sunbeam motorcycle and side car combination. It is in beautiful condition, with well-detailed spokes and, unlike the 'Expert Motor Cyclist', is extremely representative of the real machine.

when damaged, irreversibly break the whole motor.

This tinplate 'Police Convertible' (below) was made by Daiya in the 1960s and is an imaginative interpretation of a Chevrolet US police car – convertibles were certainly never regulation issue! Although the car is of tinplate, the figures are of plastic.

Mechanisms

Although Japanese firms produced some clockwork and friction-powered toys, they are best known for their innovative and imaginative use of battery power. Batteries had been used by Western toy manufacturers before World War II, but often for lighting only, and they never exploited their potential as much as the Japanese, who saw the many advantages:
* Batteries allow the toy to do complicated actions
* They enable a toy to perform for long periods
* They could be cleverly concealed. (Here, the battery box is hidden inside the side car canopy.)

Beware

Batteries can cause problems for collectors; old non-leakproof batteries can corrode, making the toy unusable, so always check for damage. It is wise to test the toy with new batteries too.

Condition

These toys were produced in much higher numbers than pre-war toys, so condition is all-important. Many have articulated parts, which,

* Interestingly, military vehicles were no longer popular by this time, having been superseded by more exciting and noisy police cars and fire engines - this one has a loud wailing siren.
* It is fitted with a clever 'mystery action' device. This was an ingenious idea invented by the Japanese, using a pair of rotating wheels under the base of the vehicle which makes the toy turn to the left or right at regular intervals and pull away from an object after a collision.

Trains

Noisy and colourful, this train (bottom) was extremely popular with young children (aged between 5 and 10 years) and vast quantities were produced. Toy trains were perennially popular and many smaller companies copied the basic shape, producing trains in different colours and sizes.

Boxes

The box can represent one third of a toy's value; their appeal stems from the elaborate illustrations which often have little resemblance to the actual toy inside.

JAPANESE NOVELTY TOYS 1945-1970

A Nomura lithographed tinplate, plastic and fabric-covered toy, McGregor the smoking Scotsman; 10in (25cm) high; 1960s; value code H

Identification checklist for Japanese novelty figures between 1945 and the late 1960s
1. Is the toy battery-operated?
2. Is it a novelty subject?
3. Does it have ingenious devices?
4. Is it marked, possibly in two different places?
5. Is the construction flimsy?
6. Does it have a hesitant movement?
7. Is it in good condition (see below)?
8. Is there an On/Off switch?

Novelty toys
Of all Japanese toys, novelty toys, capable of performing up to three or four, often complicated, movements, are possibly the most fascinating! McGregor, the 'Smoking Scotsman', in the main picture, was made by Nomura, one of Japan's largest toymakers, in large numbers during the 1950s and 1960s and it has many features typical of all novelty toy:
* A complicated battery-operated mechanism: McGregor manages to puff on his cigar, producing smoke out of his ears, while also standing up and then sitting down again.
Features include:
* The toymakers' trademark ('TN' for Nomura) is on the rear of the battery box and the American distributor's mark

(Rosko) is on the box lid.
* A jerky, hesitant movement.
* A colourful box.
* Made of inexpensive materials, which easily disintegrate. Look out for faded and cracked fabric. Sometimes small, irreplaceable parts are missing too, which lowers the value.
* McGregor is a similar character to 'Charley Weaver', a comic drunk who appears to pour liquor out of a flask and swallow, which causes his face to turn red and smoke to come out of his ears! It was based on a character created by American comedian, Cliff Arquette, who appeared on radio and TV in the 1940s.

The tinplate and fabric panda bear (above right), which smokes and shines its shoes, was made in the 1950s by Alps Shoji (founded

in 1948). It has all the typical features of novelty figures, but is an unusual version of a toy more commonly found modelled as a clown or a little boy.

Celluloid

Plastic and celluloid are materials closely associated with the Far East, although they originated in America in the 19thC. Celluloid, initially the trade name for a mixture of nitro cellulose (or Pyroxylin) and powdered camphor, was patented in the United States in 1869 by the manufacturers, Hyatt Brothers, in their quest for a substance suitable for the manufacture of billiard balls.

Celluloid toys were not common until the late 1940s, so the celluloid 'Tumbling Animal' (above) by Kuramochi is extremely rare. Light and fragile, the monkey has a simple clockwork mechanism which enables it to somersault backwards.
* It is unusual to see these types of toys in such good condition; the light celluloid is often punctured or blistered.

Plastic

'Fred Flintstone's Flivver' (above right) was made in the early 1960s by Louis Marx (1921-1980), the largest toy manufacturers in the world during the 1950s, and whose Japanese subsidiary, Linemar, manufactured many popular toys.

By the late 1950s companies

began to develop the use of plastic and use it more regularly. Fred's 'Flivver' (above), combining plastic and tinplate, is a good illustration of this transition:
* Made of lithographed tinplate, the 'Flivver' is of the same high quality as earlier toys, but Fred, cast in plastic from a simple mould, has none of the detail and marks the start of the gradual decline in quality of Japanese toys over the next decade.
* Basic in construction, its only function is to move forward and backward using a friction mechanism. This works by spinning the rear wheels by hand on the floor, which winds up a spinning flywheel to propel the toy forward when released.

Marks

Japanese toys are often marked:
* Between 1946 and 1952 marks read 'Made in Occupied Japan'. After 1952 marks either read 'Made in Japan' or 'Japan'.
* The toy is likely to be stamped with the name of the Japanese makers or with their trademark

* The box is usually stamped with the name of the American distributor (e.g. Rocks Valley or, as above, Frankonia 1965).

Collecting

Novelty toys were often originally bought by adults and kept on display. Look out for damage, such as faded fabrics and brittle plastic components.

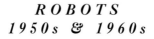

A Nomura battery-operated tinplate and plastic 'Mechanised Robot', known as 'Robbie the Robot; c.1956; 13½ in (34cm) high); value code F

Identification checklist for Japanese robots between 1950 and the 1960s
1. Is the toy battery-operated? (Batteries often carried in robot's back or in separate remote-control battery compartment).
2. Does the robot have rubber hands and a plastic-domed head?
3. Does it have a slow walking movement?
4. Does it have an On/Off switch?
5. Is it imaginatively designed?
6. Is it well-made, using good-quality body pressings and lithography?
7. Is it noisy and does it have aggressive actions?
8. Is the toy capable of ingenious tricks?

Robots

The appearance of the toy robot coincided with one of the single most important developments of the 20thC – space travel, which began in earnest in October 1957 when the first Sputnik satellite orbited the earth. In response to these technological advances and the subsequent craze for pulp science fiction, Japanese toymakers gave full rein to their creative talents, creating a wide range of robots and also space toys (see p.138).

Robbie the Robot

One of the most famous robots produced was 'Robbie the Robot' shown in the main picture, a character from the movie 'The Forbidden Planet' (1956). Rather surprisingly, the movie is based on William Shakespeare's play, 'The Tempest', starring a young Leslie Nielsen!

Although various models of Robbie were produced, such as 'Robbie Space Patrol', a combination of a robot and a space buggy, this Robbie is one of the best-known versions and has many of the robot's typical features:
* rounded limbs
* a friendly appearance (some robots are aggressive-looking)
* a transparent plastic domed 'head' – this example is in good condition, but they are prone to cracking, which lowers the value
* battery-operated pistons in the dome (or the head), which can extend and retract
* batteries in the legs.

Mechanisms

Made by Horikawa (founded in 1959), this 'Rotate-O-Matic Super Astronaut' (below left), has a more sophisticated, combined mechanism than Robbie; it walks, stops, rotates and, at the same time, its chest compartment opens and a gun fires!

Early robots, made in the

1940s are small and have simple clockwork mechanisms. During the 1950s, robots grew in size and became capable of increasingly sophisticated effects powered by complicated electric and friction-powered mechanisms.
* Typical of robots of the late 1950s and 1960s, the 'Super Astronaut' is aggressive and extremely noisy. Its warlike character is highlighted in the colourful box, depicting the robot in a violent battle scene.
* Batteries ran out of power very quickly, making them expensive to run. Consequently, although they were mass-produced, robots were generally considered to be luxury toys.

Astronauts

Astronauts are distinguished from robots by a human face beneath the helmet. Although they often perform similar actions, they are less popular with collectors.

This astronaut (below) was made in the late 1950s by Nomura. Note the fine detail on its oxygen pack and the design of its space suit.

* Its batteries are held in a remote control battery box, unusual but necessary, because its legs are too thin to hold them.

Collecting

Robots are extremely popular with collectors, but it is difficult to find them in good condition. Robots were easily damaged; they tended to walk into walls or fall over, as they were often top-heavy – and they were usually thrown away as soon as they broke. Look out for rusty chrome details too.

SPACE TOYS
1950s & 1960s

A Masadaya 'Space Giant' flying saucer floor toy; mid-1950s;
10in (25cm) wide; value code F

**Identification checklist for Japanese space models
between 1950 and 1970s**
1. Is the model made of thick tinplate?
2. Does it have a simple construction?
3. Is it brightly coloured and attractively lithographed?
4. Are batteries used to motivate it?
5. Does it have a mark (see below)?
6. Is it heavy?
7. Does it have a thin plastic window?

Space toys
Space toys, such as rocket ships, flying saucers and inter-planetary vehicles, were mass-produced by Japanese toy makers in the 1950s and 1960s. In the 1950s, space exploration was still in its infancy, and space toys, such as the 'Space Giant' in the main picture were inspired by science fiction rather than by reality.
* The 'Space Giant' is an inter-planetary space craft, possibly

heading for Saturn (this planet is depicted on the tail). As with robots, the more imaginative and fantastic space craft are in design, the more desirable they are to collectors today.

Mechanisms
Although space toys may look as if they should be flying round the solar system, sadly they are nearly always earth-bound, without as many devices as found in robots.

138

The 'Space Giant' in the main picture is a battery-operated floor toy, capable simply of moving around by means of a mystery action device – a gyroscopic wheel under the toy, which allows it to move in one direction for a few seconds, before automatically changing direction. The 'Space Tank' (below left) has a similar movement, but is friction-powered and from the late 1950s.

Made by Daishin in the late 1960s, this tinplate battery-operated toy (below) completes the transition from fantasy to reality. Commonly known as the 'American Eagle', the toy's full title is 'No. 8011 NASA Apollo II American Eagle Lunar Module' and it is closely based on the real American space exploration craft.
* This toy is capable of seven complicated actions (see box): an automatic open and shut hatch, flashing lights, revolving antennae and even 'lunar sound'.

This unusual space toy by Mansei (HAJI) (above) is a wonderful combination of Japanese space fantasy and 1950s suburban America. The driver is of the same design as used in toy cars and comes complete with check shirt and tie – not very suitable for driving a high-tech 'space car'!

As space technology became more advanced, space toys changed in response. Although this lunar space model by Horikawa (below) from the 1960s is imaginary, its name 'NASA Space Station' reflects the rise of public awareness of institutions such as NASA (America's National Aeronautical Space Agency).

Collecting

Realistic space toys are not nearly as popular as the earlier fictional versions, which have much more appeal. The box of the lunar module would have originally appealed more to adults than children and its technical accuracy would be more appropriate to a scientific model than a toy.

TRAINS 1945-PRESENT

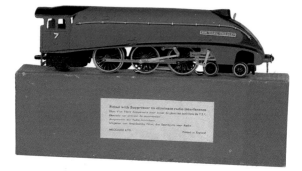

A Hornby-Dublo 'Sir Nigel Gresley' locomotive (with tender not shown), c.1952

The effects on society of World War II were as devasting as those of the Great War and these trickled down to the toy train industry. In Germany, the industry had been severely crushed and, although it did eventually recover, it was never able to recapture its pre-war strength. '0' Gauge trains made by companies such as Märklin reflected the drabness of the era and, although the range maintained its sturdy practicality, they are not the most sought after range today.

The main development for Märklin was the change from '00' Gauge to 'H0' Gauge in 1948, giving their models a more realistic appearance. In the 1950s, Märklin began to use plastic in their tenders; the use of plastic then developed and by the late 1960s metal bodies were used only for special series of locomotives.

Märklin still produce trains today, they are of a very high standard and are very popular. New trains are already a major collecting field, although it is impossible to say if they will ever increase in value as much as earlier versions have.

In America, where the war did not have such a profound effect on the toy industry American Flyer and Lionel saw a massive growth in production in the 1940s, with their Standard Gauge range as popular as ever. Their trains were packed with various exciting features too, such as electrically-powered cattle loading ramps, chimneys that produced steam and stations that could be realistically lit up. In their heyday, in the early 1950s, the companies, American Flyer and Lionel seemed untouchable. However, many new companies set up in competition, producing inexpensive and ready-to-run 'H0' Gauge trains. As a result, the popularity of Lionel's and American Flyer's more expensive ranges plummeted and the latter closed quickly in 1966.

In Britain, the early post-war period was dominated by the Hornby-Dublo range. The most interesting period to collect is between 1945 and 1953, when Hornby produced a wide range of attractive and locomotives and accessories.

Although Britain nationalised the railways in 1948, Hornby did not produce trains in British Rail livery until 1953. As a result, some pre-1952 locomotives in the liveries of the four major British railway companies are very collectable today, particularly when they are still in original boxes.

In addition to their Dublo range, Hornby continued to produce trains in '0' Gauge. In 1946 they entirely redesigned their '0' Gauge range and also changed their name from 'Hornby Series' to 'Hornby Trains'. Although sturdy and well-packaged, these trains were not of the same quality as pre-war issues; the tinplate is often lightweight, cheaply produced and of poor quality.

However, the success of the Dublo range made it impractical to continue with '0' Gauge and by the 1960s it was downgraded to a 'starter' system. In 1969 the Hornby Railways Collectors' Association was formed to promote the range, making it even more popular now with collectors than when it was originally produced.

The Hornby-Dublo range continued to be manufactured until 1964. They were popular at the time and have remained so, although they were not always of a consistently high standard. A major development in Hornby-Dublo's history took place in 1957 with their last major, and ultimately doomed, investment project. This involved upgrading their toy trains to a two-rail system and redesigning all their locomotives and stock. They continued to use diecast metal for most of the bodies, but they changed over to a high-quality plastic for freight stock and used both plastic and tinplate for passenger stock. The end product was beautifully made but too highly priced for the market place in the early 1960s. Triang, which had launched a TT miniature range of trains in 1959, were enormously successful and in 1964 they were able to take Hornby-Dublo over.

However it was not the end for Hornby; Triang had sold many of the Hornby dies (used for moulding) to G.& R. Wrenn of Basildon, which developed the range under its own name. Triang-Hornby closed in 1971 and their Triang-Hornby range became 'Hornby Railways', which still thrives today in an increasingly competitive and narrow market for model railways.

Bassett-Lowke also continued to produce toy trains until 1969. Their production was split between the lithographed tinplate range produced by George Winteringham, later known as 'Precision Models', and high-quality hand-built locomotives designed and made by Bassett-Lowke's freelance engineers, Victor Hunt and Victor Reader. In 1964, however, Bassett-Lowke closed their world-famous shop on High Holborn and the original company finally ceased trading in 1969.

Other collectable British makers of this period include Trix. Originally founded in Germany, it later moved production to Britain. The Trix Twin locomotives were especially innovative, as two locomotives could be independently operated on the same electric track.

HORNBY '0' GAUGE 1945-1969

*A clockwork Hornby train LNER 101 tank passenger set;
c.1951; '0' Gauge; value code H*

**Note: The range of toys is so vast that it is not possible
to provide a single, definitive checklist.**

Hornby in 1945

By 1945, much of the tooling
used for Hornby trains was worn
from use over many years and
many parts had been lost to war
production. The train in the main
picture was made from adapted
pre-war tooling and is typical of
their early post-war range in that:
* The locomotive is an updated
M3 model, but will be found
marked 'type 101' or '501' on the
bunker back.
* Shortage of nickel for plating
meant that this locomotive has
unusual blue coloured 'Brunofix'
coupling rods.
* Post-war coaches have pale grey
roofs and matt rather than glossy-
coloured chassis sub-frames.

Hornby Trains

In 1946, Hornby took the enormous step of redesigning their
'0' Gauge train range. The name
was changed too – from 'Hornby
Series' to 'Hornby Trains'.
Although sturdy and well-packaged, these trains were not of the
same quality as pre-war issues.

The No.20 boxed goods trains set
(above) made between 1954 and
1966 illustrates the disadvantages
of the range: the tin is very lightweight, it has been cheaply
produced and is of poor quality.

Decline

The success of the Hornby
Dublo range made the continuation of the '0' Gauge impractical
and by the 1960s, it was downgraded to a 'starter' system.

BASSETT-LOWKE
'0' GAUGE 1945-1969

A Bassett-Lowke six-coupled Southern Railways tank locomotive; c.1948; '0' Gauge; value code G

Re-issues

Bassett-Lowke's post-World War II '0' Gauge range was initially re-issued in pre-war liveries, such as this tank locomotive in the main picture.

'Flying Scotsman'

While the production of special order ships and industrial models thrived, railway production was split between the lithographed tinplate range produced by Winteringham (later known as 'Precision Models') and the high-quality hand-built locomotives that were made by Bassett-Lowke's two freelance engineers.
* The Flying Scotsman produced during this period was one of their most successful models It is seen in the picture below in its rarest and most valuable livery, c.1951-52, when British Rail experimented with blue rather than green livery.

Steel-bodied range

The budget end of the market was supplied by the 'Prince Charles' locomotive from 1951 onwards, which was produced in a range of liveries.
* A range of tinplate rolling stock was also available, such as the 'blood & custard' British Rail coaches and freight stock.

Closure

In 1964, Bassett-Lowke closed their shop on High Holborn and the company ceased trading in 1969. Today, the company have been revived, in a different form, making model traction engines and steam lorries.

Collecting

The hand-built, top-of-the-range locomotives, which were expensive in the 1950s, are still very collectable, but the lithographed tinplate range is less sought after.

HORNBY-DUBLO
1938-1964

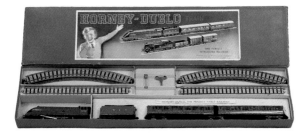

A clockwork Hornby-Dublo DP1 LNER
'Sir Nigel Gresley' passenger set; 1939; 18in (45cm); value code E

Identification checklist for clockwork Hornby-Dublo train sets 1938-1964
1. Does the train have a mechanism, either clockwork or electric?
2. If clockwork, does the train have the correct track (without a third rail)?
3. Does the locomotive have full skirts over the wheels?
4. Is the box in original condition?
5. Are the wheels and bogies free of wheel fatigue?
6. Does the train include the correct articulated coach set?

Hornby-Dublo
The success of the Märklin and Trix '00' Gauge systems inspired Meccano Limited to design their own version, which they launched in 1938, naming it Hornby-Dublo.

Far superior to the versions produced by Märklin and Trix, Hornby-Dublo trains were beautifully designed, with detailed diecast bodies. One of their first issues was the Sir Nigel Gresley locomotive and tender in the main picture.
* Hornby's chief electrical engineer, Ronald Wyborn, pioneered an efficient permanent magnet mechanism, enabling the trains to change direction easily without the need to change the motor polarity and without any mechanical switching.
* Disadvantages of the Dublo system included a clumsy three-rail design, similar to Märklin's, and Hornby did not manage to avoid the problem of diecast fatigue, which particularly affects the wheels and bogies.
* Clockwork versions have well

engineered miniature motors, and were designed as cheaper alternatives to electric ones until 1941, when production of clockwork stopped forever. As a result, they are at a premium today.

Pre-war
Hornby-Dublo trains from before World War II are difficult to find today and can be easily distinguished from later versions:
* Pale blue boxes with date codes (there are also a few surviving items issued in 1946 with pre-war boxes).
* Horizontal hook and eye coupling made of blued steel. The post-war coupling is known as a Peco coupling and has vertical bent hooks.
* Pre-World War II sets were available only in landscape format boxes (following the style of Trix). Post-war boxes were made in different shapes.

1945-1954
The Hornby-Dublo range did not nationalise until 1953. Southern Railway trains are the most popular today with collectors and this

Southern tank goods set (below) is worth much more than the London Midland & Scottish (LMS) version.

1953-1957
Once Hornby had nationalised the liveries of their trains, in 1953, they entered their most productive period, making vast numbers of good-quality (but unimaginative) tinplate freight

stock, coaches and locomotives. This EDP 12 King Passenger train set (below) is typical of Hornby-Dublo's production during the mid-1950s.

It features an up-to-date A4 Sir Nigel Gresley locomotive in green British Rail livery together with old LNER coaches, updated in Eastern Region livery.

1957-1964
In 1957 Hornby-Dublo began to upgrade and entirely replace their range, producing some of the finest Dublo models built, such as the 'Dorchester' and the 'Ludlow Castle'.

Decline
Meccano was taken over by Triang in 1964. Although production of a few plastic accessories was briefly continued by Triang (under the name Triang-Hornby), they were not of the same quality as before and the range was discontinued.
* With many minor livery and casting variations, early-post-war Hornby-Dublo trains and accessories are an interesting subject to collect.
* However, it is worth noting that it is often difficult to find Hornby-Dublo trains in pristine condition and pieces often suffer metal fatigue.

'Canadian Pacific'
One of the more exciting trains produced was this extraordinary 'Canadian Pacific' train set made between 1957 and 1958.

Hornby-Dublo were sufficiently confident in their marketing skills to believe that Canadian children would buy a British

black-painted 'Duchess of Atholl' locomotive, with a cow catcher and the 'Canadian Pacific' name added as concessions.
* Available as a freight or passenger set, the 'Canadian Pacific' was a financial disaster. Therefore, today, it is all the more sought after.

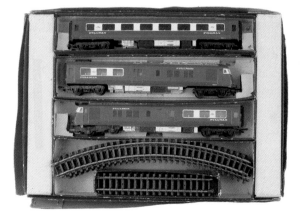

*A Triang Railways British Rail Western Region Pullman
car set in original box; c.1963; '00' Gauge; value code E*

Identification checklist for Triang Railways 1948-1971
1. Does the locomotive have a plastic body?
2. Are the power cars and coaches made of plastic?
3. Does it have an original box?
4. Is the box in good condition?
5. Does it have a hook coupling?
6. Is the train modelled on a contemporary train?
7. Does the train have an electric mechanism?
8. Is the train complete and undamaged?

Triang Railways
In 1946 Alexander Vanetzian created Rovex, a plastic company based in Richmond, Surrey, producing inexpensive toy cars and trains.

In 1950 they launched a range of two-rail electric railways. Although the track was set on an unrealistic grey plastic base, keen pricing and a lack of a third rail meant that they soon became a major rival to Hornby and Trix. In 1951, Rovex was absorbed into the Lines Brothers' Triang firm.

TT range
In 1959 Triang introduced the TT miniature range of trains in an attempt to develop the market.

Of similar appearance to '00' Gauge trains, but smaller, Triang's range was never developed enough to satisfy demand and production ceased in the mid-1960s. It is worth noting the following points:
* Always avoid incomplete sets as they are far less collectable.
* Although Triang sets lacked much of the quality found in Hornby-Dublo, they were less expensive than Hornby and also full of inventive features.
* Popular products included the 'Minic Motorway' and locomotives such as the long-running 'Princess Elizabeth' and the Pullman car set (main picture).
* Other examples included: wagons that exploded; flying helicopters; battle wagons; and a '00' scale electric slot-car system.

Hornby takeover
The success of Triang had led to financial problems for Hornby-Dublo and the Meccano group and led to a takeover by Triang in 1964. Nearly all Hornby's dies, locomotives and stock were passed to a separate company, G & R Wrenn, which continued to produce collectors' versions of Hornby-Dublo trains until 1993.

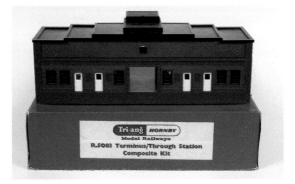

Tri-ang HORNBY
Model Railways
R.5083 Terminus/Through Station
Composite Kit

Stations

Among the few items Triang used from Hornby was the tooling for this station kit (above), making it exceptionally rare:

* Originally produced by Hornby in a sand colour, it was coloured red by Triang, along with their distinctive red box.
* It is interesting to note that the box carries a Hornby-Dublo reference number.
* Produced during 1964 only.

Other collectables that span the Triang-Hornby period between 1964 and 1971 include:
* Stephenson's 'Rocket'
* The Great Western Railway 'Lord of the Isles' locomotive
* Battle of Britain Class 'Sir Winston Churchill'.

Ringfield Motor

One of Triang-Hornby's finest locomotives was produced in 1971, using the powerful Ringfield Motor, which Triang acquired when they purchased Hornby (see also p.142).

This 'Evening Star' (below) is also an early example of tender drive – where the motor is placed inside the tender, so that the detailing of the locomotive can be more accurately modelled.
* Unfortunately, Triang went into receivership in 1971, making this one of the last locomotives that they developed.
* The new Hornby Railways Company was founded after Triang's closure and carried on the train range to the present day.

Collecting

Triang is one of the less expensive toy train fields. It is important to select items in original boxes and in good condition, such as these wagons (left). Most items from the early period, 1949-1952 are not yet collectable, apart from various pieces of British Rail Southern Region stock.

MÄRKLIN TRAINS
1945-PRESENT

A Märklin Swiss-outline 'Crocodile' locomotive CCS 800;
c.1952; 'H0' Gauge; value code E

Identification checklist for Märklin '00'/'H0' gauge locomotives 1945-present?
1. Does the train have a diecast metal body?
2. Is it marked with the serial number CCS 800?
3. Is the locomotive complete?
4. Does it have its original box (with wooden inserts)?
5. Is the locomotive heavily built?
6. Does it have 'Märklin' cast underneath?

Märklin
Märklin resumed production after World War II, in 1947. Many accessories, coaches and wagons were continued in the same style as before. The SK 800 locomotive (opposite, top) continued to be produced, for example, but with variations to the tender and locomotive body until 1952.
* All models had a slightly flatter less varnished finish with a new form of hook and eye coupling.

'H0' Gauge
In 1948, Märklin changed the scale of their models from '00' to 'H0' Gauge, giving a more realistic appearance and rendering their locomotives narrower in relation to their length.

New range
In the late 1940s and early 1950s, Märklin revised their range, with more detailed diecast bodies and displaying them in strong cardboard boxes with wooden packing pieces, such as the box in the main picture. One of the most popular models produced was the Swiss-outline 'Crocodile' articulated locomotive in the main picture, which, although highly priced, was more affordable than their pre-war '0' Gauge version (see p.84).
* Although still operating a three-rail system, by the late 1950s Märklin once again dominated the German and international market with an unrivalled reputation for consistency and solidity.

Some of the most sought-after diecast sets of the early 1950s were diesel or electric 'treibwagen' (express railcar units), such as the ST 800 (opposite, bottom). All the bogies were connected to the motor by a series of wormed gears and the set was therefore both fast and powerful, making it particularly appealing to collectors today.
* The coaches and power car are joined by finely detailed Jacobs trucks linking the two sections with a powerful spring clip, allowing maximum articulation.

Freight and passenger stock were produced by Märklin in vast quantities in the 1960s and 1970s. Many items were produced with the German Railway (Deutsches Bundesbahn) livery, as well as many pieces for export.

Collecting

Dedicated collectors are only interested in Märklin pieces in fine condition, or which are particularly rare issues.
* Märklin have always thrived by marketing their toys as premium products. Their trains always have been, and still are, expensive when bought new and, although it is not possible to predict whether material purchased now will appreciate greatly in the future, it is likely that they will at least hold their value and are a reasonably safe iinvestment.

Plastic

In 1956, Märklin began to use plastic in their tenders. The use of plastic developed and by the late 1960s metal bodies were used only for special series, such as the Hamo range of locomotives.

This Trans Europe Express set (below) was made in 1970. With its crisply detailed and attractive plastic body and handsome box, it represents the high quality of material that is still produced by Märklin today.

TRIX TWIN

*A Trix Twin 4-4-0 Hunt Class 'Pytchley' locomotive and tender;
1955; '00' Gauge; value code A*

**Note: The range of trains is so varied that it is not
possible to give a single, definitive checklist.**

Trix Twin
Originally established in 1934 in
Germany by Stefan and Franz
Bing, Trix developed a British
company with Winteringham,
Bassett-Lowke's manufacturing
arm. They were later renamed,
'Precision Models'.

Post-war range
After World War II, Trix responded to the problems of shortage of
material and a more competitive
market place by trying to increase
their export side, which they successfully achieved. Other typical
features included:
* Range mainly comprised variants of the standard four-coupled
mechanism and consisted of tank
locomotives, freight locomotives
and tenders, all in British Rail
livery, and, in addition, two
American-outline models.
* The Trix Twin Hunt Class
'Pytchley' locomotive in the main
picture has many features typical
of Trix Twin's production during
the 1950s.

German production
Trix Twin also had access to the
original German factory, with
many parts German-sourced.
Their production consisted of the
Trix Express range of trains to
complement the British range.

Features
Faced with increasing competition from Hornby-Dublo, Trix
tried to capitalise on unusual
products, such as a mineral con-
veyor wagon, and accessories,
including a large elevator loader.
* Trix also continued to produce

many of their pre-war issues, such
as this 'Many Ways' station set
(below), which comprised separate blocks, which could be
joined together to make up a
complete railway station.

Decline
After various financial problems,
Trix were taken over in 1958 by
Dufay Ltd, which abandoned the
'Trix Twin' name. Production
continued, however, and the late
1950s saw the production of some
of their finest locomotives: the
British Rail Class 7MT Pacific
'Britannia' in 1959 and the EM1
Bo-Bo electric locomotive, now
both highly collectable.

Takeover
In 1962 ownership passed to
Courtaulds. In 1967 the Anglo-
German 'British Trix' company
was formed; this takeover herald-
ed a new production phase of
high-quality plastic-bodied locomotives and stock. The English
factory finally closed in 1973,
while the German holding company still produce 'N' Gauge
miniature models today.

MODERN '00' &
'H0' GAUGE TRAINS

A Hornby Railways School Class 'Stowe' locomotive and tender;
1980; '00' Gauge; value Code A

**Note: The range of trains is so varied that it is not
possible to give a single, definitive checklist.**

Hornby Railways
In terms of volume, the new and
second-hand market for '00'
Gauge trains has been dominated
by Hornby Railways since the
early 1970s.

Many models, such as the well-
detailed Schools Class 'Stowe' in
the main picture, made in 1980,
are of a far higher quality than
Märklin and Hornby trains produced in earlier years.
* Current Hornby Railways products are now marketed towards
the adult collector.

Other makers
Numerous British and also
Continental makers have produced a wide range of Euopean-
outline locomotives since the
1960s. Among the most important
makers are the Italian firm,
Rivarossi, which produce models
of 1940s articulated steam locomotives, such as the Union Pacific
'Big Boy', as well as Fleischmann,
RoCo, Liliput (who now own
Trix), Jouef, Mainline, GMR
(Great Model Railways) as well
as Airfix.
* Märklin still produce fine-quality trains too, along with the two
important Swiss manufacturers,
HAG and Fulgurex.

Japan
In the 1960s several Japanese and
Korean companies produced a
range of highly-detailed brass
locomotives, which featured
American outlines.
* Major makers included
Tenshodo and KTM.

Subminiature gauges
Although Triang's miniature TT
gauge failed to succeed in the
1950s, subminiature gauges,
known as 'N' and 'Z' Gauge are
still popular today. Makers
include Arnold, Fleischmann,
Märklin and Minitrix.

G. & R.Wrenn
After Hornby-Dublo were taken
over by Triang in 1964, George
Wrenn, bought much of the old
Hornby tooling and dies and used
them to manufacture two-rail
locomotives and stock, often in
variations and liveries not
achieved by Hornby. Today, these
are some of the more valuable
modern trains available. One of
the main reasons for this was the
retirement of George Wrenn in
1992, and the subsequent closure
of the factory. Much of the stock
and machinery was bought by the
English railway company, Dapol,
which continue to make Wrenn
trains alongside their own in a
museum in North Wales.

Collecting
Model railway production is
aimed at adult collectors and is
increasingly distant from the traditional children's toy railways.

Improvements in technology
mean that lightweight, plastic
trains, such as those produced by
Bachmann, contemporary
American toymakers, are of a
quality and detail not possible
only a few years ago and it is
likely that they will eventually
become very collectable.

LEAD FIGURES
1945-PRESENT

A Britains' 'Picture Pack' series French Foreign Legion Officer, 1959

When World II ended, the production of lead toy soldiers was slow to restart in the United Kingdom, as the Government's restrictions on lead prevented the use of this commodity for the home market. The only toy soldiers available during the late 1940s were for export only. By 1949, however, production was again in full swing, and, although some pre-war companies had not survived the war years, other new makers were to emerge as important players in this field

Britains deleted many of their pre-war lines and replaced them with more up-to-date sets, mainly depicting ceremonial troops of the United Kingdom, Europe and the USA. Most pre-war boxes had been given the label, 'Armies of the World'; this was changed post-war to 'Regiments of all Nations'. In the USA, dimestore soldiers were reissued, while, in France, figures by Mignot continued to be produced, but, in Germany, manufacture had temporarily ceased, owing to the closure of the Elastolin and Lineol factories during and just after World War II.

The Coronation of Queen Elizabeth II, Cinemascope epics and the advent of BBC Children's Television programmes brought forth an enormous flood of figures and manufacturers were keen to depict characters and events from the period. Initially only produced in lead, by the early 1950s plastic toy soldiers and figures were starting to emerge as the newest and most exciting toy figures for children.

Advertised as 'unbreakable' they were shortly to take over from lead figures completely. A British company, Herald Miniatures, produced some superb plastic toy figures during this period, a fact not overlooked by Britains, which incorporated the company in 1953. This was a far-sighted move in anticipation of the day when lead would not be considered suitable for children's toys. By the early 1960s the government was already considering banning lead from toys and increasing numbers of toy soldier manufacturers were turning to plastic.

Timpo and Charbens, for example, all changed to plastic during the mid-1950s and by the time legislation was passed in 1965, all makers, including Britains, were deleting lead toys from their range.

Continental companies were also producing plastic figures by now, with Starlux of France and R.E.A.M.S.A. of Spain of particular importance. In America, Marx, renowned for their toy-making activities in other fields, produced unpainted figures in plastic and included them in a box called 'Playsets', which comprised tinplate buildings and accessories, accompanied by soldiers and figures.

It was during the early 1970s that toy soldier collecting changed direction and became more of an adult rather than a children's hobby or pastime. Many collectors wishing to recapture the pleasure obtained from their toy soldiers from childhood started to collect the figures which were no longer available in lead.

A steady second-hand market for these items started to emerge, culminating in what was possibly the most important collection of toy soldiers ever to be auctioned, the Britains Company Archive Collection, at Christie's South Kensington, in June 1994.

Toy soldier collecting also developed in another direction, with the production of 'new' metal soldiers made of white non-toxic metal from the early 1970s onwards. Britains, simultaneously with a firm named Blenheim, conceived the idea of producing 'new' toy soldiers which would be compatible with the now obsolete hollow-cast figures.

This term is now recognised as a form of collecting for the adult, rather than the child. As with Britains' early figures, many other companies have emerged and the number of firms supplying 'new toy soldiers has grown steadily over the past 20 years.

Almost any period of history or type of toy soldier is available for collectors today, with non-military figures currently the most popular. Britains once again started to package their 'new' toy soldiers, or 'new' metal models as they are known, in their traditional red boxes, and extended the range in the early 1980s in a series of boxed limited editions.

A set quantity of a particular regiment was produced each year, allowing collectors not only to buy sets which were new on an annual basis, but to ensure the investment potential of deleted sets year by year.

HOLLOW-CAST LEAD
FIGURES 1945-1966

*Two Wend-al 'Toytown' figures; early 1950s;
2in (54mm); value code H*

**Note: The range of figures is so vast that it that it not
possible to provide a single, definitive checklist.**

Post-war developments
Lead figure production after
World War II was slow to restart.
It was not until 1949 that the
UK government lifted restrictions on the use of lead for
making children's toys. When
they were lifted, at first it was
only to supply the export market.

Many of the major companies,
including Britains, John Hill &
Co., Charbens, Crescent and Taylor
& Barrett, had all survived the war
by turning their resources to war

production. Several new companies emerged too, some operated
by ex-servicemen using their
pensions to invest in toy-making
ventures. Of the new firms,
Timpo (Toy Importers) became
Britains' main post-war rival,
while Segal, Sacul, Luntoy and
Wendal became successful too.

The Coronation, 1953
Although the years following the
end of World War II were a time
of austerity for Britain, the toy

industry was given an enormous boost by a series of well-timed events, which helped to revive interest in toy figures.

The Coronation of Queen Elizabeth II in June 1953 provided a major marketing opportunity for all toymakers. In commemoration, Britains re-issued, with minor alterations, their pre-war Coronation state coach (bottom), used for King George VI's Coronation in 1937.
* The coach was available either as a single piece or in various boxed display sets.
* The eight horses are harnessed by wire traces.

New issues

Many of the sets of foreign troops produced by Britains before World War II became obsolete with the creation of new nations and states after the war and were deleted to make way for new designs. As a result, these issues are highly sought after today. Other Britains series included:
* Knights of Agincourt (both on foot and mounted).
* boxed sets of soldiers, depicting ceremonial troops from the Changing of the Guard, the Household Cavalry Musical Ride and the Sovereign's Escort.

Timpo

In addition to their own version of the Coronation coach and attendants, Timpo produced a very successful range of figures based on the Cinemascope epics of the early 1950s.

The figure of Sir Lancelot (below left) comes from the Knights of the Round Table series produced in the 1950s. Also available were characters from Ivanhoe, Quentin Durward and other MGM epics.
* Timpo also produced a series of American GIs in action and in bivouac poses.

Other makers

John Hill & Co.were not slow to cash in on the cinema epics either and made a large set based on the film, Quo Vadis. BBC Children's Television was also becoming an important influence on the young during the early 1950s, and makers such as Sacul and Luntoy quickly secured the rights to reproduce characters in lead from the puppet shows broadcast during Children's Hour, including 'Muffin the Mule' and 'Sooty'.

Aluminium

In a departure from hollow cast, Wend-al also produced a series of 2in (54mm) scale figures in aluminium, in an effort to issue figures that could be described as unbreakable. They made a variety of subjects, including the Toytown soldier in the main picture, from the early 1950s, dressed in Napoleonic uniform.

Decline of lead

By 1960 the British government had banned lead in children's toys. This had a disastrous affect on toymakers, leading to the closure of Luntoy, Sacul, John Hill and Segal, Taylor, Barrett, Charbens and Cherilea.

Lead production was scaled down to a minimum by Britains and by the early 1960s it was used only in figures exported to North America. Timpo made its final lead figures in 1956, and was the first to change over to full-time plastic production. Britains had foreseen the emergence of the plastic toy figure and had, during the course of the 1950s, taken over Herald Miniatures, leading plastic toy figure makers, thus giving them a head start in the plastic figure market.

PLASTIC FIGURES
1950-1980

A Herald Miniatures plastic Guardsman Standard Bearer; 1952;
2in (54mm) high; value code A

Note: The range of plastic figures is so vast and varied, that it is not possible to provide a single, definitive checklist.

Herald Miniatures
Although manufacturers had experimented with plastic for several decades, it was not until the 1950s that the first plastic figures were produced in large quantities, by Herald Miniatures.

They made a wide range of figures, such as the Guardsman Standard Bearer in the main picture. Other figures included khaki troops, Lifeguards and cowboys and indians.

Britains
Quick to realise the future importance of plastic in toymaking, Britains decided to incorporate Herald Miniatures into their own

company in 1953 thus giving them an important inroad into the plastics market. By the early 1960s, nearly all Britains' figures, such as Robin Hood, historical soldiers and Polar explorers, were made of plastic.

One of the most successful ranges was the 'Eyes Right' series of ceremonial figures of guardsmen, Infantry of the Line and Royal Marines.

Bands were also introduced, including US Army and Marine bands.
* The figures were so-named because they had moveable arms and heads, enabling them to adopt the 'Eyes Right' position!

Britains Swoppets

Swoppets were a highly successful series of knights, cowboys, indians and infantry, which had moveable heads and arms and interchangeable bodies, heads and equipment.

The knight (above) has a moveable visor and weapons, which, as the name suggests, could be swopped with those from other figures.

Deetail (1974-present)

In 1974 Britains first made the Deetail series of figures of solid plastic with metal bases, such as this Union Officer (above).
* They also made Guardsmen, Foreign Legion soldiers, Arabs,

Mexicans, 8th Army and Africa Korps, in addition to World War II Japanese soldiers.
* A range of Super Deetail figures followed in 1982, which featured paratroops and UN troops.

Timpo

Timpo changed to plastic production in 1956 and, at first, simply re-issued figures from their lead range. Later, they adopted a simpler version of the Swoppet idea and made figures with interchangeable parts, such as the Roman soldier (below, left):
* Cowboys, indians, Mexicans, German, US and British World War II troops and Vikings were also produced.
* Timpo survived until 1979, when they were forced to cease trading, leaving Britains as the only remaining British manufacturers of toy soldiers.

France

Starlux (1950-1992) made many figures, mainly based on modern

French armed forces or periods from French history, such as this Napoleonic Marshal (above).

Other countries

* Elastolin were relaunched in the 1950s and made 3in (65mm) scale toy soldiers, including modern soldiers, in plastic until 1984.
* Louis Marx in America made sets of plastic figures with the emphasis on large 'playsets', including buildings and equipment to complement the figures.

Condition

Plastic figures are made of self-coloured plastic over which paint is added and they can sometimes become brittle with age.
* This results in flaking, and plastic figures are seldom found in mint condition.

'NEW' TOY SOLDIERS

A Britains' limited edition set of different soldiers from the Cheshire Regiment; 1984; 2in (54mm) scale; 1984; value code A

Identification checklist for Britains' 'new' toy soldiers 1972-present
1. Is the figure solid and of white metal?
1. Is it 2in (54mm) high?
2. Does it have a thick green diecast base?
3. Is the figure glossily painted?
4. Does it bear the name of a particular manufacturer on the underside of the base?
5. Is the figure part of a set?
6. Does the box have a label on it indicating that it is limited edition?

New toy soldiers
Since their introduction in the 1970s, collecting 'new' toy soldiers has been predominantly an adult hobby, sometimes for pleasure and sometimes for potential investment.

Over 200 manufacturers have produced 'new' toy soldiers over the past 20 years, resulting in a healthily competitive market.

The ranges of figures and the periods of military history produced by these companies are far more comprehensive than those issued by the former toy soldier-making companies. Most new manufacturers can be classed as cottage industries, mainly run by members of the maker's own family; with casting, painting and packaging taking place at home.

Britains

In 1972 Britains introduced a selection of solid-cast figures made from non-toxic white metal into their range to satisfy the growing demand from collectors. The range developed, and in 1983 Britains produced their first limited edition boxed sets, and are still producing them today.

Six or seven thousand sets of a particular regiment are produced each year and once the limited quantity is sold out, the investment potential rises. The set in the main picture was one of the first produced, in 1984, and because it is still in excellent condition, its value has risen almost ten times since then.

* The 'Special Collectors Edition' boxed set of Sherwood Foresters (at the bottom of the page) was made by Britains in 1993. Note its superb condition.

* Following this success, Britains have added unlimited sets and individual figures based on the hollow-cast range, giving rise to a whole new generation of collectors.

Other companies

Many new companies also realised that new toy soldiers were becoming a lucrative field, keenly collected by adults. The most notable companies include Trophy, Ducal and Blenheim.

Subjects

Many new toy soldier firms try to establish their own unique ranges. They look to uniform details of present day ceremonial troops, or uniforms from periods of military history or battles to come up with exciting ideas for their ranges.

Over 40 such manufacturers are currently producing soldiers throughout the world and in so doing cover almost all periods of military history in their designs.

Collecting

New toy soldiers are big business, and, as new ranges are introduced and deleted, figures became instantly collectable.

Condition is paramount to the value. Toy soldiers produced today in limited quantities might well be future investments, but this cannot be guaranteed.

TINPLATE TOYS
1945-PRESENT

A Betal clockwork lithographed tinplate trolley-bus, c1945-50

World War II had an enormous impact on the international toy industry. In 1939, after nearly one hundred years of supremacy, Germany was still the world's leading toymaking centre. By the end of the conflict, in 1945, Germany's economy lay in tatters and its most valued overseas customers were looking elsewhere for fresh outlets of toys.

One of the most unexpected and important developments in the toy industry in the early part of this period was the rise of Japan as a powerful and influential economy. Both Japan and Germany were under Allied Occupation between 1945 and 1952, but the Japanese still managed to seize some of the toy market from established European centres and earned a reputation of their own as the centre for innovation and imaginative designs.

To compound Germany's problems, the war had taken its toll on some of their most sucessful toymakers. Few new German toymakers were set up after World War II either, although leading firms, such as Märklin and Schuco, continued to produce successful and good-quality tinplate toys. Other successful makers from this period include well-established names such as Günthermann, Tipp, Arnold, Gama, Gescha, Kellermann and Technofix.

Initially in this period lithographed tinplate continued to be the most widely used material, with clockwork still the most popular mechanism. All the traditional subjects were covered too, such as cars, lorries, fire engines, boats, aircraft and novelty figures, but military vehicles fell out of fashion, as in all countries.

Of particular interest to collectors are German tinplate character figures. These clockwork figures depict ordinary workers, such as farmers or dockers, carrying out their daily activities. What is of particular interest to collectors and historians are their distinctively determined faces, reflecting the resolution to rebuild Germany's economy.

By the 1950s these toys had become much more light-hearted. As Germany began to enjoy a healthier economy, its toys reflected the new affluence; faces on figures are usually more content in appearance, while vehicles represented the most luxurious models of the day. This can be clearly seen on the lithographed images on tinplate family saloon cars, which depict happy a driver and passengers on the windows, often with the family dog too. These designs are often American-influenced.

Although German toys were of equivalent quality to those from pre-war years, the recent war between Germany and the Allies still lingered in popular memory. In consequence, traditionally loyal customers, such as Britain and France, preferred to buy domestically-produced toys.

This patriotic streak is particularly evident in British tin-plate toys, with a national campaign in the late 1940s which encouraged people to 'Buy British'. Toys were convenient tools for advertising this message, and it is common to find tinplate toys emblazoned with patriotic slogans. These advertising hoardings were probably aimed as a selling point towards the parent who was purchasing the toy, rather than at children. The late 1940s trolley-bus in the main picture is a typical example, displaying advertisements for 'Bisto' gravy, 'Palm' toffees and 'Shredded Wheat' cereal. Although many vehicle types were produced, those representing buses or trains were particularly popular in the early post-war years, when large numbers of people did not have their own cars, and relied on public transport far more than today.

British tinplate toys varied greatly in quality in the early post-war years. One of the best-known tinplate toy makers of this period was Triang, founded as an offshoot of the Lines Bros. family toymaking business in 1919. Having successfully survived World War II, they continued to produce their very popular tinplate Minic series of toy vehicles until 1963. Other major British makers of this period include Meccano and Chad Valley.

Meccano Ltd. continued to produce Meccano Constructor sets, although they were becoming less popular popular. Available with red and green components in a selection of sets and accessory outfits, they were advertised and featured editorially in the monthly Meccano Magazine. Dinky Toys and Hornby-Dublo trains increasingly became Meccano's most successful sales areas (see Chapters Seven and Nine).

At one time the most important material for making toys, tinplate was gradually superseded as the toy market developed in the post-war era. The success of the diecast technique played an important role in the development of inexpensive and attractive toy vehicles, but, by the late 1960s, plastic – cheaper to produce and safer for children – that had almost made tinplate redundant.

BRITISH TINPLATE
1945-PRESENT

A Triang Minic tinplate fire engine, made between 1945 and 1952;
5¼ in (13.5cm) long; value code G

Identification Checklist for Triang Minic vehicles
1945-early 1950s
1. Is the vehicle made from several parts joined
together with metal tabs (see below)?
2. Does it have black rubber tyres (most pre-World War
II vehicles have white tyres)?
3. Does it have die-cast hubs (these were less
expensive to produce than pre-war chrome hubs)?
4. Is it similar in design to a pre-war vehicle, but
without electric headlamps?
5. Does it have original paintwork?

Triang (1919-present)
Triang was founded in 1919
as an offshoot of the Lines family
toymaking business. In 1935, they
started to produce a range of
small vehicles in the Minic series.
Unlike many companies which
collapsed during World War II
when their factories were turned
over to arms production, Triang
managed to survive and continued to make a wide range of
Minic toys until 1963.

Main features
The fire-engine above has several
features typical of many post-war
Minic vehicles:
* more deeply-coloured than
the pre-war versions (the range

of models available was smaller),
* designed to a scale sufficiently
accurate to allow it to be incorporated into the popular '0' Gauge
railway lay-outs of the day,
* fire engines were a popular
theme, along with police cars
and buses, replacing military
vehicles as the most popular type
of action toys,
* good-quality parts (sometimes
vehicles have parts made pre-
1939, shelved during the war
and reconstructed after 1945),
* clockwork mechanism (later
models were fitted with a 'Push
and Go' flywheel friction drive),
* a colourful, well-illustrated box
(some toys were sold in boxed
presentation sets too).

Marks

Triang always marked toys with a gold-coloured triangle or embossed mark (representing the partnership of the three Lines brothers).

Buying British

After the end of World War II there was a growing enthusiasm for buying British products. After the dominance of German toys in the 1930s, British toys saw an upsurge in popularity, becoming a symbol of patriotism.

Typical of the period is the advertisement hoarding 'Thanks for buying British' on this bus (below) by Wells (1919-1965), often known as Wells o' London. Notice how it is marked with the name 'National Service' – a state-run company.

* Period details are very appealing – note the pipe smoker on the upper deck and how many people are wearing hats!

Packaging

Paper shortages after the war meant that packaging was often basic, as with this box (below) by Chad Valley (1825-present), where a new label has been carefully pasted over a box from another model.

Chad Valley had established a strong reputation for tinplate toys during the 1930s, but this clockwork buffet car made c.1951 shows a marked decline in the quality of lithography.

Tinplate decline

This tinplate policeman (below) by Mettoy (1936-83) is a particularly vivid example of the decline of British tinplate toys from the 1950s onwards.

* The policeman has a simple mechanism – he sways from side to side. A basic toy, this piece is of low value.

* Mettoy was founded in Britain 1936 by Philip Ullmann, head of the German company, Tipp & Co, after he had been forced to leave Germany. In 1956, they introduced the Corgi Toy range (see p.118).

Plastic toys

By the 1960s plastic toys had largely superseded tinplate. Inexpensive to produce, durable and safe, plastic toys were frowned upon by some adults, but were popular with children.

Television became an important part of children's lives and, quick to seize the opportunity, toymakers produced a wide range of TV-related toys. This plastic 'Stingray' (above) by Lincoln International, made in c.1963, is based on the submarine from the Gerry Anderson TV series, 'Stingray'.

GERMAN TINPLATE
1945–PRESENT

A painted tinplate fire engine by Schuco c.1961;
12in (30cm) long; value code D

Identification checklist for Schuco vehicles 1945-78
1. Does the toy have a mark (see below)?
2. Is it of good quality?
3. Does it have a solid construction?
4. Is it finely finished with no protruding parts?
5. Does the paint have a glossy finish (the vehicle would have been sprayed several times, as with actual vehicles)?
6. Does it have many novel features?

German post-war toys
Germany, the world leader of toys since the early 19thC, faced new challenges after the end of World War II. Many countries, such as Britain, who had fought against Germany, now had greater opportunities to market their own toys, while in the Far East, Japan was quickly establishing itself as the centre for innovative and imaginatively designed battery-operated toys.

Although few new toy companies started up after the war, leading firms, such as Märklin and Schuco continued to produce successful, good quality toys. This fire engine in the main picture by Schuco, made in 1961, illustrates the high standard of toys available and has many features typical of post-war Schuco toys:
* a well-made box with fitted inner compartments
* many accessories

* excellent details (this fire engine comes with an extending ladder escape on a turntable and electric lighting). It is battery-operated, whereas most German toys made in the 1950s were still powered by clockwork.

The lithographed tinplate 'Merry Clown' (below) is a typical clockwork toy of this period. Made c.1951, it is an attractive toy, well-lithographed in bright colours.

Marks

All Schuco vehicles were marked on the base plate. Early post-war models, between 1945 and 1952, are marked 'Made in US zone Germany' and, from 1952 onwards, 'Made in Germany'.

Technique

Most post-war German figures were made of painted tinplate. This traffic policeman, 'Flic' by Schuco (below) was made in 1954 of diecast metal, and is therefore extremely rare and desirable.

* This rare 'Cabrio' clockwork car by Kellermann, from the late 1940s would appeal to VW Beetle collectors, even though it is not entirely realistic in design.
* Kellermann (1910-1979) specialized in the production of penny toys, particularly tinplate animal figures.

Style

The determined expression of the dockyard worker (below) is typical of the faces of many post-war German character toys, symbolizing the country's resolution to rebuild her economy. Produced by Wüco (Wünnerlein, Fritz & Co.) in the 1950s, the clockwork mechanism is concealed in the simulated wooden crate, which tumbles over and over, pulling the man along with it.

* 'Flic' has an inventive clock-work mechanism which allows him to move his arms to wave on and stop traffic, corresponding to the colour semaphore visible in the base of the model.

Collecting

* Toy motorbikes are generally as popular with motorbike enthusiasts as they are with toy collectors, and in some cases this can help to push up prices.

Motorbikes

This novelty Arnold 'Mac' motorbike (left) from the mid-1950s has an ingenious mechanism, and is more desirable, than contemporary Japanese battery-operated versions.

Driven by clockwork, the bike moves in a circle at the same time as the rider mounts and dismounts.

MODERN TOYS
(I)

A Gilbert James Bond Action Figure of Sean Connery from the film, 'Thunderball'; c.1965; USA; 12in (30.5cm) high; value code G

Note: The range of toys is so vast and varied that it is not possible to give a single, definitive checklist.

Modern toys

Today, toys are made in vast numbers all around the world. In addition to some of the long-established makers, such as Märklin and Britains, there are countless companies and factories mass-producing a wide variety of toys of varying quality.

The Far East has remained the major toy production centre since the end of World War II, with companies such as Tomy, Tonka, Asahi and Yonezawa. Quality varies enormously, from inexpensively-produced plastic figures which cost only a few pounds to high-quality, high-price items.

Europe and America have seen a different pattern emerging, with a wealth of simple wooden and soft toys geared towards learning. * Successful makers include Galt of Britain (see also p.78), Fisher-Price and a large number of toy artists, who work at home producing fine-quality, individual toys.

Such is the enormous range that it is possible to illustrate only a few of the most interesting and representative modern toys, all those which are now collectable.

Action figures

Action figures by makers such as Louis Marx, Gilbert and Pelham, along with various factories in China, have recently become collectable, but only if they are in good condition and complete with the figure's original box. Of particular interest to collectors are 'character' figures, such as the James Bond action figure in the main picture.
* Other film characters were depicted from the series 'Captain Scarlet', 'Stingray', 'Fireball XL-5' and 'Thunderbirds'.
* The Bond figure is plastic, with a spring-operated arm, which shoots a cap-firing pistol. (The gun is missing from this piece.)
* Made by Gilbert, the American firm based in Connecticut, active in the 1960s and 1970s.

TV-related items

Television has played an increasingly important part in children's lives over the past 30 years. Popular programmes often resulted in spin-off products, such as this Dr.Who Dalek (below) made in 1964 by Louis Marx, under licence from the BBC.

The Dalek is typical of the high standards of many of their toys. Made of good-quality moulded plastic, it has a battery mechanism enabling it to emulate the full-sized Dalek movement.

Dan Dare

Already an established collecting-field in America for several years, classic comics and related items from the 1940s and 1950s have recently seen an enormous rise in popularity in Britain and Europe. The major collecting area within this field are extremely rare comics (usually mint condition first editions) and related artwork. The most collectable comics are 'Superman' and 'Batman' from America and the British 'Eagle'.

Various spin-off toys featuring characters from the comics, such as Dan Dare from 'Eagle' were produced too.

This toy 'Dan Dare Radio Station' was made during the late 1950s and early 1960s and is keenly sought after by today's Dan Dare enthusiasts.
* The station has an attractive two-colour printed, corrugated cardboard box with an attractive 'comic-like' graphic illustration.

Japan

This 'bullet train' was made in the late 1960s in Japan for the American makers, Tonka Toys (Mond Metalcraft Ltd.) founded in 1946. Tonka became well-known for their sturdy and durable toys.

* This unusual train (left) depicts the Japanese Railways' 'Hikari' Express train.
* It is still fairly presentable and with some value, although it has clearly been well-played with.

MODERN TOYS
(II)

unified colour. The cube-shaped puzzles were produced in vast quantities and are of little value today, even if they still have their original box and instructions.

This globe version (above), known as Rubik's 'World Puzzle' was produced only in 1982 and now is much rarer and more collectable than cubes today. It is 4in (10cm) high with the stand.

Rupert Bear
The success of the Rupert Bear comic strip in the *Daily Express* newspaper, first published in 1920, and the subsequent Rupert Bear annuals led to a wealth of Rupert Bear souvenirs and novelty toys. This bagatelle game made in the 1970s is of particular interest as it features all the major characters.
* Note how Rupert is depicted as a brown bear in this coloured game; he is always shown as white in cartoons.
* Bagatelles were also made featuring other popular children's characters of the day, such as 'Noddy', 'The Magic Roundabout' and characters from 'Camberwick Green' and 'Mickey Mouse with Friends'.

Puzzles
New puzzles and brain-teasers became increasingly popular with both adults and children during the 1970s. Of varying quality, many are now of little value. The most successful puzzle produced was the Rubik's Cube, invented by the Hungarian mathematician, Erno Rubik. The standard version of the puzzle was indeed cube -shaped, with different coloured squares on the sides – the aim was to twist each moveable side to make each side one

The space toy above is called 'Dingbot' and was designed by another Japanese toy firm, Tomy (1924-present) and made in Singapore. Its features include:
* Battery-operated with a 'bump n' go' action, which allows it to waddle forward, stop periodically and produce squeaking noises.
* Friendly in appearance, compared with the robots of the 1950s and 1960s (see p.136).
* Practical and easy to clean
* Boxes are tight fitting and are easily damaged.
* Introduced in the late 1980s, it is still available today, so it is difficult to speculate if it will become collectable. It is possible

that it will, as it is so well made and designed, reflecting the best of the toys produced at the end of the 20thC.

Space toys
Contemporary developments in the world of space and technology continue to be a popular theme with toymakers. These two N.A.S.A. 'Enterprise' Space Shuttles (below) were produced c.1979 by Masudaya of Japan. Although they are well-made, they are less exciting and imaginatively designed than earlier Japanese space toys from the 1950s and 1960s (see p.138).
* Battery-operated and made of lithographed tinplate and plastic.
* The 'deluxe' silver version is remote-controlled with hand-operated steering actions; the white version has an automatic

turning movement and flashing red and green lights.
* They are also have a very loud noise action!
* One of the last tinplate toys produced in Japan, the quality of the lithographed tinplate is high, but the lower body plastic components are simple and unimaginative. By the early 1980s, nearly all toys were made of plastic worldwide.

Collecting
It is impossible to speculate accurately on future collectable toys, as trends and fashions change so readily. Collectors are always on the look-out for new fields, so the best advice is to follow the contemporary toy market carefully by regularly visiting major toy retailers, auctions and markets and to buy what appeals to you.

McDonald's toys
One of the most successful series of licensed toys of the past decade has been the series of promotional toys (a selection is shown below) produced for the McDonald's hamburger

restaurant since 1984. Available with their 'Happy Meals' as an attraction to children, they are made both for the America and European market.
* Issued in sets of four or six, with new ones made regularly.

* Made of plastic, the toys usually have several moulded components attached with inset screws.
* Carefully designed to be colourful and to have no rough edges
* Other hamburger restaurants, such as Burger King, offer similar toys, but these are not yet as popular.

SELECTED TOYMAKERS

Page reference in brackets refer to fuller entries given elsewhere. Please note that makers' marks always appear *underneath* the relevant text entry.

Richard & Karl (Carl) Adam (estab'd 1893)
An East Prussian company, specialising in tin toys, acquired by Lehmann.

Alemanni (estab'd 1908)
Italian makers of tinplate toys.

Alps Shoji Ltd. (estab'd 1948)
Manufacturers of various types of tinplate novelty toys.

Althof, Bergmann & Co. (estab'd 1867)
A New York-based company involved mainly in commissioning toys, although they did make some too. One of the first American companies to make carpet trains, their trademark was 'A.B.C.' (registered in 1881).

American Flyer (estab'd in 1907)
Based in Chicago, USA, and made a range of toy trains, both in cast iron and tinplate.

Arnold (estab'd 1906)
This German firm's major success was the introduction of sparking flint toys. They also produced a range of novelty toys and boats.

Asahi Toy Co. (estab'd 1950)
A large Japanese company, producing novelty and spacetoys, such as robots, with battery-powered actions.

Asakusa Toy Ltd. (estab'd in 1950)
Japanese makers of various types of tinplate novelty toys with battery-powered actions.

Automatic Toy Works (estab'd in 1868)
Early American manufacturers of clockwork toys.

Bandai (estab'd 1950)
Japanese makers of novelty toys and tinplate vehicles.

Bassett-Lowke (estab'd in 1899)
Founded by the Englishman,

Wenman Bassett-Lowke, this company became a major force in toy train industry, both commissioning trains from companies such as Bing and Carette, and later manufacturing them via Winteringham. They also ran a shop on High Holborn London, which closed in 1964.

Bell (estab'd 1919)
Makers of mechanical tinplate novelty toys and vehicles.

Biller (estab'd 1937)
Based in Nuremberg and makers of toy railways and novelty toys. Trademark was a large letter 'B' with a clockwork key.

Bing, Gebrüder (1879-1933)
Based in Nuremberg and made tinplate toys, particularly cars, boats and trains, as well as railway stations and accessories.

Bird & Sons (estab'd 1870s)
An English firm based in Birmingham, which made tinplate toys.

Blomer & Schüler (estab'd 1919)
German toymakers, which initially produced clockwork mechanisms for other makers, but later changed to making a wide range of tinplate novelty toys.

Bolz (estab'd 1875)
German makers of seaside toys and spinning tops.

Bonnet et Cie (estab'd 1912)
A French, which acquired Fernand Martin in the 1920s. Made clockwork novelty toys and vehicles and tinplate figures.

**Bowman Models Ltd.
(estab'd late 1920s)**
Britsh manufacturers which specialised in '0' Gauge live-steam
toy locomotives and trains.

Brianne (estab'd c.1889)
French makers of high quality tinplate railways. Also imported Bing
and Carette trains.

**Brandstätter, Georg
(estab'd 1877)**
German makers of tinplate toys
and children's prams.

Braglia (estab'd 1913)
Italian manufacturers, producing
small toys, aircraft, construction
sets and Gauge '0' trains.

Brimtoy Ltd (estab'd c.1912)
British makers of inexpensive tinplate trains and toy vehicles.
Trademark was Nelson's Column.

**Britains Ltd., William
(1860-present)**
British makers of lead figures
from 1893 and particularly famous
for perfecting the hollow-cast
techniqe of moulding figures.
World leaders in toy figure production from the late 19thC to the
present. Mark cast in horses from
1900, labels on foot soldiers and
figures replaced by lettering cast
into base from 1905.

**Brown, George W.
(active 1856-80)**
Based in Forestville, Connecticut,
USA. Specialised in mechanical
toys. Became the Stephens &
Brown Manufacturing Co. in
1868, making tinplate toys.

Karl Bub (estab'd 1851)
Nuremberg-based makers of tinplate toys, some with clockwork
mechanisms. Acquired Gebrüder
Bing in 1933.

Bucherer, A. & Co (estab'd 1945)
Based in Switzerland and
specialised in making model railway for the European markets.
Trademark was name 'Buco'.

Bühler (estab'd 1860)
Germany suppliers of clockwork
mechanisms to a large number of
toy manufacturers.

Burnett Ltd. (estab'd c.1905)
British makers of tinplate vehicles.
Were acquired by Chad Valley ,
large toy manufacturers in Liverpool
(q.v.) in the late 1930s.

**Butcher & Sons Ltd.
(estab'd 1920)**
English manufacturers of toy cars
and construction kits. They were
also known under their trademark,
'Primus Engineering'.

Ettore Cardini Co. (1922-1928)
Italian manufacturers specialising
in tinplate toys.

**Carette & Cie., Georges
(1886-1917)**
Carette was a Frenchman based in
Nuremberg. His company was
among the first in Europe to introduce electric trains as well as a
range of cars, boats and railways.

Chad Valley (1823-present)
Trade name of Johnson Brothers,
based in Birmingham, England.
Made tinplate toys and selfassembly toys.

Chein (estab'd c.1903)
One of the first American companies to develop the use of lithography and manufacturers of tinplate vehicles and novelty toys.

**C. I. J (Compagnie Industrielle
de Jouets) (1902-1964)**
Makers of model cars for Citröen
and Renault and diecasts in the
1950s and 1960s.

André Citroen (estab'd 1923)
Sold top-quality promotional models of Citroen cars, made for them
by C.I.J. until 1936.

Crandall, Charles M., and Jessie A, (1840s-1905)
Based in New York. The company patented a tongue-and-groove system of flat printed wooden blocks in 1867. Produced a series of wooden toys with interlocking and interchangeable parts.

Dinky Toys see Hornby

Distler & Co., Johann (estab'd late 19thC)
Based in Nuremberg and made tinplate vehicles, penny toys and comic characters.

Doll & Cie (1898-1938)
Based in Nuremberg and made steam engines and novelty toys. Were taken over by Fleischmann in 1938.

Dowst Company (1890s onwards)
A Chicago publishing house which, began to produce diecast 'crackerjack' toys, and later, the more sophisticated Tootsie Toys (see p.110).

Dunbee-Combex-Marx (1972-1980)
Based in the USA, at one time they were the world's largest toy manufacturers, having acquired Schuco, Marx and Lines Brothers.

Dux (Markes & Co.) (estab'd 1904)
German makers of construction kits, best known for their 'Astroman Robot'.

Hans Eberl (estab'd c.1900)
Germany makers of novelty toys and tinplate vehicles.

Gebüder Einfalt (estab'd 1922)
Makers of novelty toys, later became Technofix.

Essdee (estab'd 1920)
German makers of tinplate toys.

Falk, J (estab'd 1897)
German makers of magic lanterns and steam-powered toys.

Fallows & Son. J.M. (1847-1900)
From Philadelphia in the USA, they made boats and horse-drawn vehicles in tinplate.

Fischer, Georg (estab'd 1903)
Makers of mechanical tinplate toys. Trademark was an intertwined 'G.F.'.

Fischer, H. & Co.
Based in Nuremberg, they made various tinplate toys.

Gebrüder Fleischmann (estab'd 1887)
Nuremberg-based manufacturers which specialised in making toys, boats and model trains.

Förtner & Haffner (1922-1927)
German producers of tin soldier 'flats', solids and small novelty toys. They were acquired by Bing in 1927 and later became Trix. Their trade name was 'Anfoe'.

Francis, Field & Francis (1838-70s)
Also known as the Philadelphia Tin Toy Manufacturing Company. Produced a range of tinplate toys and dolls' house furniture.

**Fuchs & Co.
(active in the 19thC)**
Nuremberg-based makers of tin-plate toys and musical instruments.

**Geyper S.A. Industrias
(active in early 20thC)**
German makers of tinplate toy cars and conjuring sets.

Greppert & Kelch (Gundka-Werke) (estab'd c.1900)
Based in Brandenburg, Germany, they made small tinplate toys.

Günthermann (1887-1965)
Based in Nuremberg, they made clockwork toys and fine hand-enamelled novelty toys.

**Haji Mansei Toy Co.
(estab'd 1951)**
Japanese manufacturers of model tinplate cars.

Hausmann, E (active c.1910)
Based in Nuremberg, they made steam engines, trains, and tinplate novelty toys. Were also whole-salers for other toymakers.

**Hausser O. & M.
(estab'd 1910)**
Based in Ludwigsburg, Germany, and made tinplate military vehicles and composition figures under the tradename, Elastolin.

Heyde (1840-1945)
Based in Dresden, Germany, they made semi-solid and solid lead figures and boxed sets of soldiers. Their work is widely copied.

Höffler (1938-1947)
German makers of tinplate clock-work toys.

Horikawa Toys (estab'd 1959)
Japanese manufacturers of novelty toys and space toys. Trademark was 'S.H.' in a diamond.

Hornby, Frank (1863-1936)
An English toymaker, who was behind Meccano toys from 1901, Hornby trains from 1920 and Dinky Toys from 1933.

**Hubley Manufacturing Co.
(1894-1940s)**
Based in Lancaster, Pennsylvania and made cast-iron toys, banks and gun caps.

**Ichiko Kogyo Co. Ltd
(active 1950s-1960s)**
Japanese makers of tinplate toys, particularly cars.

Issmayer (estab'd 1861)
Makers of novelty toys and trains.

Ives, Edward Riley (1868-1928)
Established a factory in Plymouth and, later, Bridgeport, Connecticut, USA. Made cast-iron and tin toys. Was absorbed by Lionel, 1928.

J.E.P. (Jouets de Paris)
A French firm, founded as the Société Industrielle de Ferblanterie in 1899. Renamed Jouets de Paris in 1932. Specialised in tinplate toys.

Kanto Toys (estab'd c.1950)
Japanese makers of lithographed tinplate novelty toys with clockwork mechanisms.

Kellermann, Georg & Co. (estab'd 1910)
Based in Nuremberg and originally made penny toys. Later, they made simple mechanical toys.

Köhnstam (estab'd 1876)
Founded by Moses Köhnstam (hence trade name) and were major German toy distributors.

Lehmann, Ernst Paul (1881-present).
Established company in Brandenburg, Germany. Early tin toys had flywheel mechanisms, later versions had clockwork. (See also p. 66).

Lesney (1947-present)
A British company, which introduced the Matchbox series of miniature diecast vehicles. Most clearly marked 'Lesney', 'Matchbox' or 'Moko'.

Lineol (estab'd 1923)
Based in Brandenburg, Germany and made military toy vehicles and composition figures. These are similar to Hausser's 'Elastolin' range, but more finely detailed.

Lines, G & J. (active 19th-20thC)
A London-based company which made wooden rocking horses and hobby horses. Created Triang in 1919. Also made wooden toys, pedal cars and, from c.1930, made metal cars. Trade marks were 'Triang', 'Triangtois' and 'Minic'.

Lionel (1901-1950s)
Based in New York and New Jersey, USA. As the Lionel Manufacturing Company, they made toy trams and trains, and, from 1908, train sets. Produced Disney toys from 1934.

Löwenstein, Herman (estab'd 1918)
Swiss makers of high-quality model electric railways.

Lütz, Ludwig (estab'd 1846)
Founded in Ellwangen an der Jagst, Germany. They made tin carriages, train sets and dolls' house furniture. Märklin took over the company in 1891.

Mangold (estab'd 1882)
Based in Furth, Germany and made toys under licence to Schuco (q.v.) in the late 1940s.

Märklin (1859-present)
Famous German toymakers, producing high-quality vehicles, novelty toys and locomotives.

Martin, Fernand (1878-1912)
A Parisian company which reputedly made over 800,000 tin toys a year. Were taken over by Victor Bonnet et Cie in the 1920s.

Marx, Louis (estab'd 1920-1982)
By the 1930s, the American firm, Marx, were the largest toy manufacturers in the world.

Meccano see Hornby

Mettoy Co. Ltd (1936-1983)
A British company, founded by
Henry Ullmann, former proprietor
of Ferman Tipp & Co. Made tinplate Mettoy toys between the
1930s and 1950s and diecast Corgi
toys from 1956.

Mignot (1825-present)
French manufacturers of solid, flat
and some hollow-cast figures.

**M.T. (Modern Toys)
(estab'd 1924)**
Japanese makers of tinplate, celluloid and, later, plastic toys, many
with battery-operated mechanisms.

Nüsslein(estab'd 1899)
German makers of humming tops,
magic lanterns and musical boxes.

Paya (1880s-present).
A Spanish company, making tinplate toys, particularly cars and
'0' Gauge trains. Toys still
produced as collectors' items.

**Péan Freres
(active in the late 19C)**
French makers of all types of toys.

Plank, Ernst (1866-c.1935)
An instrument-making company
based in Nuremberg, working in
tin and brass. Produced 80,000
steam engines, ships and trains in
1899. Steam-driven cars were
made from 1904.

Reed Toy Co., W.S. (1876-97)
Based in Leominster,
Massachusetts, USA. Made wood-
en toys, such as ships, decorated
with lithographed paper.

Rock & Gräner (c.1830-1905)
German makers of tinplate toys
and trains.

**Rossignol, Charles
(c.1868-1962)**
A French company which produced floor trains, cars, boats and
a famous series of Paris buses.
The trademark 'CR' appears on
nearly all toys.

Rouissy (estab'd 1920s)
French makers of clockwork and
electric railways. Their trademark
was 'L.R.'

Schönhut, Albert (1872-c.1935)
The 'Humpty Dumpty Circus'
registered in 1902 was the company's most successful product (see
also p.78).

**Schreyer & Co. (Schuco)
(1912-1978)**
Made clockwork figures with tinplate bodies in plush or felt and
'one-piece' tinplate cars. Also
made motorcycles.

**Shephard Hardware Co.
(1866-c.1892)**
Based in Buffalo, New York and
produced tin toys and cast-iron toys.

**Schroed r & Co.
(active in the early 20thC)**
German makers of steam engines.

**S.F.A. (Société de Fabrication et
d'Assemblage) (estab'd 1936)**
French makers of tinplate toys.

**Stevens & Brown Manufacturing
Co., (1843-c.1930)**
Based in Connecticut. Best-known
for cast-iron toys and banks.

Stock & Co. (estab'd 1905)
German makers of tinplate toys
(often imitated the style of
Lehmann's toys).

Taiyo Kogyo Ltd. (estab'd 1959)
Japanese makers of robots, space
toys and novelty figures.

Tipp & Co. (1912-71)
A Nuremberg-based company,
which made tinplate cars and
comic character toys.

T.N. (Nomura Toys) (estab'd 1923)
Japanese makers of tinplate
robots, novelty figures and space
toys. Prolific after World War II.

Trix (1927-1973)
Based in Germany, they produced
construction sets and electric
trains. A subsidiary company was
established in 1935 in Britain.

**Volkseigener Betreib Mechanic
(estab'd c.1947)**
This state firm took over from
Lehmann (q.v.) in 1948 and made
cheap imitations of earlier toys.

TRAIN GLOSSARY

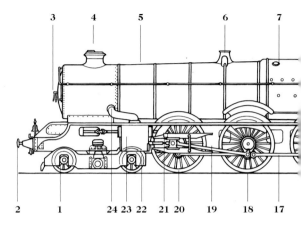

KEY TO ILLUSTRATION

1 Bogie wheel
2 Buffer and buffer beam
3 Smokebox door
4 Chimney
5 Boiler
6 Safety valve
7. Firebox
8. Handrail
9 Cab
10 Backhead (controls)
11 Tender
12 Coupling
13 Axle box
14 Axle guard
15 Cab step
16 Trailing wheel
17 Coupling rod
18 Driving wheel
19 Connecting rod
20 Leading wheel
21 Crosshead
22 Outside cylinder and piston
23 Valves
24 Main steam pipe to cylinder

TOY TRAIN GAUGES

The gauge of a train is measured from wheel centre to wheel centre.
The table below shows the different measurements of gauges.

All makers	00/H0 Gauge	⅝in (16.5mm)
''	Gauge 0	1⅜in (35mm)
''	Gauge I	1⅞in (48mm)
''	Gauge II	2⅛in (54mm)
Bassett-Lowke Bing Carette	Gauge III	2⅝in (67mm)
Märklin Schönner Bassett-Lowke Bing	Gauge III Gauge III Gauge IV Gauge IV	3in (75mm)

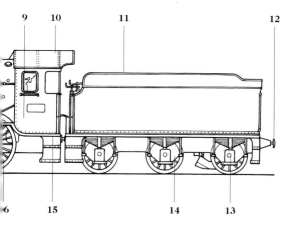

9   10   11   12

6   15   14   13

Boiler Tubes containing water that run through boiler. Heat from firebox is drawn along the locomotive, heating tubes in the process, and exhaust steam and waste is then emitted from the train's chimney.

Clerestory The raised centre section of a carriage roof fitted with windows or ventilators.

Coal rail A separate rail which runs around the top of a locomotive tender.

Connecting rod The rod which joins the coupling rod on the locomotive to the piston.

Coupling The linkage which joins carriages together.

Cow catcher A metal frame on the front of American trains to remove obstructions, such as cows, from the track.

Dribblers and piddlers Known by both names, these toy trains were made by manufacturers such as Clyde Model Dockyard in Glasgow or Stevens Model Dockyard in London, Produced in Britain from 1870-1920s.

Electric outline A train based on an electric prototype.

Firebox The heart of a locomotive, where coal burns intensely to heat water flowing through an insulated jacket around it.

Gauges The term to describe the scale in which a locomotive is made, see table opposite.

Handrail Rail for crew to hold onto during maintenance.

Private Owner Van A van belonging to a private company, and moved by the railways as part of a freight train.

Rake A group of coaches coupled to a locomotive.

Rolling stock General term for wheeled railway vehicles.

Smokebox The chamber at the front of a steam locomotive with an opening for the removal of combustion waste.

Spectacle plate The vertical plate at the front of a locomotive cab, originally with two 'spectacle' windows.

Splashers The enclosure around locomotive wheels.

Steam dome The dome at the top of many locomotive boilers, where steam is collected to be piped to the cylinders.

Steeple cab A locomotive with a steeple-shaped central cab, on electric-outline locomotives only.

Tender A special wagon that carries coal and water, located directly behind the locomotive.

Train A locomotive, tender and coaches.

Windcutter A streamlined design found on French and German locomotives, with distinctive V-shaped chimneys, steam domes, cab and boiler.

Wheel configuration The formation of the wheels on a locomotive, starting at the front. A 'Pacific' 4-6-2 locomotive has four bogie wheels, six driving wheels and two pony wheels (at the back end of the engine).

TOYS GLOSSARY

Artillery wheels Spoked wheels with a tyre of white stretched rubber (often found on German cars between 1900 and 1914).

Articulated The term describing a toy connected by joints that are sufficiently loose to allow movement in any direction.

Axle Metal rod joining two vehicle or wagon wheels

Battery-powered mechanism See Mechanisms

Bearings Metal surface or ball-race which support an axle or a crankshaft.

Bi-polar An electric locomotive mechanism first used in America in the 1920s.

Board games Games played on a specially designed card or fabric surface. The most common types of games involve players moving across the board by throwing dice and using counters to mark their position on the board.

Caboose The American term for a guard's van.

Carpet toy A toy that can be played with only on the floor. For example, a train that does not fit any standard track or a toy aeroplane that cannot fly.

Celluloid The original trade name for Pyroxylin, an early and highly flammable form of plastic used for making toys. Invented in the United States in 1869 by the Hyatt Brothers.

Chassis The separate structural frame on which all locomotives were built and most veteran and vintage cars, declining in use after the adoption of the one-piece body in the 1930s.

Chromolithography See **Lithography**.

Clockwork mechanism See **Mechanisms**.

Coal rail A separate rail around the top of a locomotive tender.

Composition An inexpensive substance made from, variously, cloth, wood, wood pulp, plaster of Paris, glue and sawdust, used for making doll's heads, bodies and limbs, as well as other toys, notably Elastolin and Lineol civilian and military figures. (See also p.106).

Construction kit A toy that comprises various components, where the aim is to join them together to build a toy, such as a car or building. One of the most famous makers of construction kits were the English firm,

Meccano, which first produced their innovative 'Mechanics Made Easy' outfits in 1901, later renaming them Meccano.

Crazing A random pattern of fine cracks in the paint of a hand-enamelled toy – usually a sign that the paint is old, but can be copied by the finest restorers.

Diecast The term for a shape formed in a metal mould under pressure. Lead was initially used as the main ingredient, but this was replaced in Britain in 1934 with mazac (a magnesium and zinc-based alloy) which was safer.

Dissected puzzle A puzzle made of a picture which has been dissected into various pieces, where the aim is to put the pieces together so that the picture is complete.

Diorama A miniature three-dimensional scene (particularly popular in the 19thC).

Electric mechanism See **Mechanisms**.

Embossed Pressed decoration on tinplate, done by a hand or steam powered press.

Fatigue A form of granular collapse of the metal of which some diecast toys are made.

Floor-runner A carpet train or toy that is propelled along the floor by a hand movement.

Flywheel A mechanism in some toys before 1914, which operates on the inertia principle, with power provided by hand or by string.

Friction power See **Mechanisms**.

Gift sets Sets of toys sold together in a box, often as a special editions; in this way, quite unexciting sets can be transformed into valuable ones.

Gunwale Upper part of the bow of a boat.

Impressed The method whereby a maker's mark is indented into the surface of a toy as opposed to raised.

Hollow-cast figures Toy figures with hollow bodies, made using the hollow-cast technique perfected by William Britain in 1893.

Incised The method whereby a maker's mark is scratched into the surface of a toy's head; as opposed to indented (see above).

Jigsaw The commonly used 20thC term for dissected puzzles; so called after the type of saw used to cut them.

Journal The part of a shaft or axle that rests on bearings.

Journal box An oil box that contains the grease to lubricate the ends of the axles.

Juvenile drama Sheets of sets, figures and dialogue for children to recreate their favourite plays at home (particularly popular in the late 18th/early 19thC).

Lacquer A hard glossy coating, often found on tinplate toys and trains, usually of shellac, a natural varnish which is derived from an Indian beetle.

Lead A main ingredient in some diecast toys until 1934; most widely used in making toy figures until the 1960s.

Lead Rot As harmful as fatigue, but affecting the alloys of which lead figures are made, resulting in a white powdery residue and eventual decay and collapse.

Leyern The German name for wooden swing toys made in the late 18thC. Also known as *kumperkisten* in the Erzgebirge area of Saxony, Germany.

Licensing The process whereby manufacturers compete to earn the right to produce toys on behalf of other companies; often associated with film and television productions.

Lining A delicate and fine line or group of lines to highlight and decorate panels on locomotives and stock and early cars.

Lithography The process by which sheets of tinplate are printed in the flat before being pressed into shapes; also applies to paper items.

Mazac A magnesium and zinc-based metal alloy regularly used in the diecast technique from 1934 onwards.

Mechanical bank A savings money box in which the depositing of coins depends on some mechanical action, usually made from cast-iron. These were particularly popular with both children and adults in the United States after the Civil War from 1869 to late 19thC.

Mechanisms The way in which a toy with movement is powered. The simplest types of mechanicism are 'push-along' and 'pull-along', where the toy is moved by hand. More complex mechanisms include:

* Live steam - usually found in boats and early locomotives; where a simple brass boiler is heated externally by a spirit lamp, with steam generating power for a single or twin cylinder engine.

* Clockwork - as the name suggests – is powered by springs of various sizes. They vary from wide, flat section boat springs made of blued steel that run for many minutes, to feeble Lehmann coiled wire springs that peter out suddenly after a frenetic turn of speed.

* Electric motors: the various types are too numerous to list, but, in brief, the early locomotive motors from the 1890s were: Alternating Current, poorly insulated and lethal in short circuit. These remained popular until the arrival of low voltage systems in the 1920s and Bassett-Lowke's 'Permag' (permanent magnet) DC motors in the 1930s. With a permanently charged field, winding, forward and reverse control became simpler, and systems safer.

* Boats were available with all power sources, with massive glass jar batteries to power the larger liners, or twin linked vertical steam engines. Most cars up to 1940 were clockwork, with a few models using batteries for the motor rather than just the lighting, mostly by the makers Bing and Bub.

* Steam was rarely used, apart from very early cars such as the Bing 'Spider', 1902 or the large and ugly Doll steam car, from the 1920s.

* Lightweight electric mechanisms became more common after 1945, particularly in Japan. Batteries were either stored in the base of vehicles or in boxes on remote control leads.

* Compact motors also allowed the creation of Scalextric in 1957.

* Friction motors at this time tended to consist of a free-spinning laminated iron disc in a simple gear toy train.

* The rubber-band mechanism is a relatively crude but effective mechanism, commonly used in toy aircraft. In most cases, the aircraft was propelled into the air for a few seconds before plunging to the floor. The manufacturers, F.R.O.G. improved on this greatly, with triple bands giving enormous power to their lightly and finely designed aircraft.

Metal fatigue A particular form of damage common to diecast toys and components produced between 1934 and 1940, whereby the metal tends to distort, crack

and crumble easily. See also
Fatigue (above).

Mint A toy that is without the slightest blemish. In reality, near-mint is the best condition in which one is likely to find a toy, even fresh from a shop. A commonly used expression is mint and boxed, used to describe toys in near perfect condition.

Model A miniature representation of a vehicle or building, made exactly to scale or to proportion. Sometimes a perjorative term suggesting that charm has been sacrificed for detail.

Nests Interlocking cardboard boxes, which are usually covered with brightly coloured lithographed paper.

Novelty toy Any non-vehicular mechanical toy which has an amusing action.

Nuremberg A famous medieval town in Bavaria in Southern Germany, where most German tinplate toymakers were based apart from Märklin.

Mystery action This makes a battery-operated toy turn to the left or right at regular intervals and pull away from an object after a collision.

Penny Toys Inexpensive toys usually made from lithographed tinplate, with a simple push-along action. Production was mainly between 1900 and the 1930s.

Plastic Synthetic material with a polymeric structure, which can be easily moulded when soft and then set. Plastic increasingly replaced tinplate as the main material with which to make toys from the late 1940s and today nearly all toys are of plastic.

Plywood A type of inexpensive laminate sometimes used to make wooden toys.

Proscenium The arch separating the stage from the auditorium in a theatre.

Reproduction The term used to describe any modern copy of an antique toy.

Robots Mechanical toys, made in the 1950s onwards, particularly in Japan, in the form of fantasy space figures capable of ingenious actions.

Ring Method Wooden animals for arks and farmyards made in Germany in the 19th/early 20thC were traditionally made using the ring method. A large circle of wood was turned so as to produce the animal in cross-section. The animals were then cut from the ring in slices. The legs were separated and details, such as the ears and horns, were added.

Rockers Curved pieces of wood, forming the base to a rocking horse, mainly used in the 19thC. See also **Safety stand** (below).

Rust A reddish-brown oxide, the main enemy of cast-iron and tin toys. The catalogue term 'surface rusting' indicates reddish bloom on the surface which is sometimes possible to remove.

'Rust spotting' is more serious, as the paint or lithography will probably have been destroyed under the spots. 'Rusted through' means that the metal has been completely eaten away.

Safety stand A stand for rocking horses where the horse is hung on metal bars from a secure wooden base, which was used from the late 19thC onwards. See also **Rockers** (above).

Scrapbooks Books compiled from pieces of decorative printed paper (scraps) and other ephemera. They were particularly popular with children and adults in the 19thC.

Screw Propeller on a boat.

Solid figures Toy figures which have a solid-cast, as opposed to a hollow-cast, body. Typically made in the 19thC by companies such as Lucotte, Mignot and Heyde.

Space toys Toys representing fantasy space vehicles and figures, such as rockets, space figures and space ships.

Spring suspension A form of suspension first used by the British diecast toymakers Corgi and Spot-On in their vehicles.

Stacks Funnels on a boat.

Still bank A savings money box which has no mechanical movement involved in the deposit of coins into it.

Swoppets A series of toy figures first produced by Britains in the 1950s, which had interchangeable bodies, heads and equipment.

Tabs A method of joining two pieces of metal by folding a small tab through a slot.

Two-tone A method of painting using two adjoining colours.

Transfers Transparent membrane stuck on to toys to depict a detail, such as advertisement panels on Dinky Toy vehicles.

Tinplate Thin sheets of iron or steel which are coated with a tin-based alloy.

Turned A term that is used of a wooden toy that has been shaped on a lathe.

BIBLIOGRAPHY

GENERAL

Fraser, Antonia *A History of Toys* Weidenfeld & Nicholson, London, 1966

Hannas, Linda *The English Jigsaw Puzzle* Wayland Publishers, London, 1966

Herts, Louis H. *The Toy Collector* Hawthorn Books/Thomas Y. Crowell Co, 1967; Funk & Wagnalls, New York, 1969

Murray, Patrick *Toys* Studio Vista, London 1968

Mackay, James *Nursery Antiques* Ward Lock, London, 1976

Speaight, George *The History of the English Toy Theatre* Studio Vista, London, 1967

TINPLATE TOYS

Ayres, William, S. *The Warner Collector's Guide to American Toys* The Main Street Press, Warner Books Inc., New York, 1981

Barenholtz, Bernard and McClintock, Inez *American Antique Toys* Harry N. Abrams, New York, New Cavendish Books, London, 1980

Harley, Basil *Toy Boats* Shire Publications, 1987

Cieslik, Jürgen and Marianne *Lehmann Toys* New Cavendish Books, London, 1982

Franklin, M. J. *British Biscuit Tins* New Cavendish Books,London

Gardiner, Gordon and Morris, Alistair, *Metal Toys* Salamander Books Ltd., London, 1984

Gardiner Gordon and O'Neill, Richard *Toy Cars* Salamander Books Ltd., London, 1985

King, Constance *Metal Toys and Automata* The Apple Press, London, 1989

Marchand,F. *Motos-Jouets, L'Automobiliste* Paris, 1985

Pressland, David *The Art of the Tin Toy* New Cavendish Books, London 1976

Tempest, Jack *Collecting Tin Toys* William Collins, London, 1987

TRAINS

Bassett-Lowke, W.J., *The Model Railway Handbook* (volumes III-XV), W.J. Bassett-Lowke & Co., Northampton, 1910-1950

Carlson, Pierce *Toy Trains* Harper & Row, NewYork/Victor Gollancz Ltd.,London, 1986

Carstens, Harold H. *The Trains of Lionel's Standard Gauge Era* Railroad Model Craftsman, London, 1964

Coluzzi, Count Giansanti *The Trains on the Avenue de Ruminé* New Cavendish Books, London/Editions Serge Godin, Paris, 1982

Foster, Michael *Hornby-Dublo Trains* New Cavendish Books, London, 1980

Fuller Roland *The Bassett-Lowke Story* New Cavendish Books, London, 1984

Graebe, Chris and Julie, *The Hornby Gauge 'O' System* New Cavendish Books, London, 1985

Louis H. *Collecting Model Trains* Mark Haber & Co., London, 1956

Hornby, Frank *Life Story of Meccano* New Cavendish Books, London 1979

Huntington, Bernard *Along Hornby Lines*, Oxford Publishing Co. Oxford, 1976

Joyce, J. *Collectors' Guide to Model Railways* Model and Allied Publications, Argus Books, Hemel Hempstead, 1977

Levy, Allen *A Century of Model Trains* New Cavendish Books, London, 1974

Reder, Gustav *Clockwork, Steam and Electric: A History of Model Railways up to 1939* Ian Allen, Shepperton, Middlesex, 1972

TOY SOLDIERS & FIGURES

Carman, W.Y. *Model Soldiers* Charles Letts, London, 1973

Garrett, John G. *Model Soldiers; A Collector's Guide*, Seeley Services, London, 1965

Garratt, John, G. *The World Encyclopedia of Model Soldiers* Frederick Muller, London,1981

Johnson, Peter *Toy Armies* B.T. Batsford, London, 1982

Joplin, Norman *British Toy Figures 1900 to the Present* Arms and Armour Press, London, 1987

Joplin, Norman *The Great Book of Hollow-cast Figures* New Cavendish Books, 1993

Joplin, Norman *Toy Soldiers* Apple Press, London, 1994

Kurtz, Henry I. and Erlich, Burtt, *The Art of the Toy Soldier* New Cavendish Books, London,1979

McKenzie, Ian *Collecting Old Toy Soldiers* B.T. Batsford, London, 1975

Opie, James *Toy Soldiers* Shire Publications, Bucks, 1983

WHERE TO VISIT &
WHERE TO BUY

WHERE TO VISIT

Britain
Abbey House Museum
Abbey Road
Kirkstall
Leeds
Yorkshire LS5 3EH

Arundel Toy and
Military Museum
23 High Street
Arundel
Nr. Chichester
West Sussex BN18 9AD

Bethnal Green Museum
of Childhood
Cambridge Heath Road
London E2

Bickleigh Castle
Bickleigh
Tiverton
Devon EX16 9RP

C.M. Booth Collection of
Historical Vehicles
Falstaff Antiques
63-67 High Street
Rolvenden
Kent TN17 4LP

Buckley's Yesterdays World
90 High Street
Battle
East Sussex TN33 OAQ

Cabaret Mechanical Theatre
33-34 The Market,
Covent Garden
London WC2E

Canterbury Heritage Museum
Stour Street
Canterbury
Kent CT1 2JE

Chester Toy and Doll Museum
13a Lower Bridge Street
Chester
Cheshire CH4 8JW

Cockthorpe Hall Toy Museum
Cockthorpe
Well-Next-The-Sea
Norfolk NR23 IQS

Cotswold Motor Museum and
Toy Collection
The Old Mill
Bourton-on-the-Water
Nr. Gloucester
Gloucestershire GL54 2BY

The Cumberland Toy and Model
Museum
Banks Court
Market Place
Cockermouth
Cumbria CA13 9NG

Dewsbury Museum
Crow Nest Park
Heckmondwike Road
Dewsbury
West Yorkshire WF13 2SA

Gloucester Folk Museum
99-103 Westgate Street
Gloucester
Gloucestershire GL1 2PG

The Haworth Museum of
Childhood
Main Street
Haworth
Keighley
West Yorkshire BD22 8DU

House on the Hill Toy Museum
Mountfitchet
Stansted
Essex CM24 8SP

Ironbridge Toy Museum
Banbury Road
Gaydon
Warwick CV35 OBJ

The London Toy and Model
Museum
21 Craven Hill
London W2

Museum of Childhood
Church Street
Ribchester
Lancs PR3 3YE

Museum of Childhood
42 High Street (Royal Mile)
Edinburgh
Lothian
Scotland EH1 1TG

Museum of Childhood
Sudbury Hall
Sudbury
Derbyshire DE6 5HT

Museum of London
London Wall
London EC2

Pickford's House Museum
41 Friargate
Derby
Derbyshire DE1 1DA

Pollock's Toy Museum
1 Scala Street
London W1

Richmondshire Museum
Ryders Wynd
Richmond
North Yorkshire DL10 4JA

The Precinct Toy Collection
38 Harnet Street
Sandwich
Kent CT13 9ES

The Sussex Toy and Model
Museum
52-55 Trafalgar Street,
Brighton
Sussex BN1 4EB

Thirlestone Castle Trust
Thirlestane Castle
Lauder
Berwickshire TD2 6RU

Tintagel Toy Museum
Fore Street
Tintagel
Cornwall PL34 ODD

The Toy Museum
Dedham Art & Crafts Centre
The High Street Dedham Essex
CO7 6AD

The Toy and Teddy Bear
Museum
373 Clifton Drive North
St Annes
Lytham-St-Annes
Lancs FY8 2PA

America
Antique Toy Museum
Exit 230, I-44
PO Box 175
Stanton, Missouri 63079

Bauer Toy Museum
233 E. Main
Fredericksburg
Texas

Sullivan-Johnson Museum
223 North Main Street
Kenton, Ohio

Nashville Toy Museum
2613 McGavok Pike
Nashville, Tennessee

Museum of the City of
New York
5th Avenue and 103rd Street
New York, NY

Museum of Childhood
8 Broad Street
Greensport, New York

Remember When Toy Museum
Box 226A
Canton, Missouri 6345

Toys and Soldiers Museum
1100 Cherry Street
Vicksburg
Missippi

Toy Train Museum
Paradise Lane
Strasburg
Pennsylvania

Washington Dolls' House and
Toy Museum
5236 44th Street, NW
Washington DC 20015

WHERE TO BUY

Auction Houses

Britain
Bonhams Chelsea
65-69 Lots Road
London SW10 ORN

Christie's South Kensington
85 Old Brompton Road
London SW7 3LD

Phillips Bayswater
10 Salem Road
London W2 4DL

Sotheby's
34-35 New Bond Street
London W1A 2AA

America
Bill Bertoia Auctions
2413 Maddison Avenue
Vineland, NJ 08360

Christie's East
219 East 67th Street
New York, NY 10021

Hake's Americana & Collectibles
PO Box 144N
Pennsylvania 17405

Mapes Auctioneers
1600 Vestal Parkway West
Vestal, NY 13850

Phillips New York
406 E.79th Street
NY 10021

Richard Opfer
Auctioneering Inc.
1919 Greenspring Drive
Timonium, MD 21093

Sotheby's
1334 York Avenue
New York, NY 10021

INDEX

PICTURE CREDITS AND ACKNOWLEDGMENTS

The publishers would like to thank the following auction houses and collectors for supplying pictures for use in this book or for allowing their pieces to be photographed.

1 CSK; 3 CSK;16 CSK 18 P; 19l PC, 19tr CSK, 19br PC;
20 PC(x 2); 21 PC(x3); 22 PC; 23tr CSK, 23l PC, 23bl PC;
24 CSK; 25 PC(x3); 26 CSK; 27 CSK(x3); 28 CNY; 29 CNY(x3);
30 CSK(x2); 31 CSK(x3); 32 CSK; 34 CSK; 35tl CSK, 35tr CSK,
35bl SL, 35br CSK; 36t CSK, 36br SL; 37 CSK (x3); 38 SL;
39tl SL, 39br CSK, 39b CSK; 40 CSK; 41tl SL, 41tr CSK, 41bl
CSK 41br CSK; 42 CSK(x2); 43 CSK(x2); 44t CNY, 44b CSK;
45 CSK(x2); 46 CSK; 48 CSK(x2); 49 CSK(x4); 50 CSK(x3);
51CSK(x4); 52 CSK; 53 CSK(x3); 54 Chris(x2); 55t CSK, 55l
Chris, 55r CSK, 55b Chris; 56 CSK(x2); 57c Chris, 57b CSK;
58 CSK; 60 CSK; 61 CSK(x4); 62 CSK(x2); 63l CSK, 63r CSK,
63b SL; 64 CSK; 65t SL, 65c CSK, 65b CSK; 66 CSK; 67
CSK(x3); 68 CSK; 69 CSK(x3); 70 CSK(x2); 71 CSK(x3);
72 CSK(x2); 73 CSK(x4); 74 CSK(x2); 75 CSK(x3); 76 CSK(x2);
77 PC(x3); 78 PC(x2); 79 PC(x3); 80 CSK; 81tr PC, 81tl PC,
81bl PC, 81br CSK; 82 CSK; 84t CSK, 84b Chris; 85t Chris,
85br CSK, 85b Chris; 86 CSK; 87t Chris, 87c Chris, 87b CSK;
88t Chris, 88b CSK; 89 CSK(x3); 90 Chris(x2); 91 Chris(x2);
92 Chris(x2); 93 Chris(x2); 94t CSK, 94b Chris; 95t Chris;
95b Chris; 96 CSK; 98 NW; 99l RW, 99r CSK; 100 RW;
101 RW(x2); 102t CSK(x2); 103 CSK(x3); 104 S&NJ(x2);
105 S&NJ(x4); 106 SJ(x2); 107tr SJ, 107l DP, 107bl SJ; 108 CSK;
110 CSK(x2); 111 CSK(x3); 112 CSK(x2); 113 CSK(x5); 114 CSK;
115 CSK(x4); 116 CSK(x4); 117 CSK(x2); 118 CSK; 119 CSK(x2);
120 CSK(x2); 121 CSK(x2); 122 CSK(x2); 123 CSK(x2); 124 CSK;
125 CSK(x3); 126 CSK; 127 (CSKx3); 128 (CSKx2); 129 CSK(x2);
130 CSK; 132 CSK; 133 CSK(x3); 134 CSK; 135 CSK(x4);
136 CSK; 137 CSK(x2); 138 CSK(x2); 139 CSK(x3); 140 CSK;
142 CSK(x2); 143 CSK(x2); 144 CSK; 145tl Chris, 145c CSK,
145b Chris; 146 CSK; 147t Chris, 147c Chris, 147b CSK;
148 CSK; 149 CSK(x3); 150 CSK(x2); 151 CSK; 152 RW;
154t S&NJ, 154b RW; 155 NJ; 156 S&NJ; 157tl AL, 157cl JW,
157bl AL, 157r AL; 158 JW; 159 JW; 162 CSK; 162 CSK;
163 CSK(x4); 164 CSKx2); 165 CSK(x4); 166 CSK; 167l CSK,
167r CSK, 167b PC; 168 PC(x3); 169 PC(x2)

KEY
b bottom, c centre, l left, r right, t top

P	Pollock's Toy Museum, London
PC	Private Collections
CSK	Christie's South Kensington
CNY	Christie's, New York
Chris	Christopher Littledale, The Sussex Toy and Model Museum
S&NJ	Sheila and Norman Joplin
SJ	Sheila Joplin
AL	Adrian Little
SL	Sotheby's, London
DP	Don Pielin
JW	John Waterworth
RW	Rob Wilson
NW	Nigel Williamson

Thanks are also due to the following for their generous help in the preparation of this book:

Miranda Marsh and Christopher Littledale

MILLER'S CHECKLISTS are designed to offer collectors a fast and accurate way to identify and date antiques within a particular specialised collecting area. Each one is written by a leading expert, and details of the authors are given below. On the final page of this book are details of a selection of Miller's titles, together with an order form.

If you would like more details about the Miller's range or wish to order further titles in the Checklist series, pease see the order form on the next page.

VICTORIANA, ART DECO AND ART NOUVEAU

Eric Knowles is a director of Bonhams, the major London auction house. A leading authority on 19th and 20th century decorative arts, he appears regularly on many television and radio programmes, including the *Antiques Roadshow*, *The Great Antiques Hunt*, *Crimewatch UK* and BBC Radio 2's *Jimmy Young Show*. His other books include Miller's *Royal Memorabilia* and *Victoriana to Art Deco*.

FURNITURE

Richard Davidson is a BADA (British Antiques Dealers Association) furniture dealer in Arundel, West Sussex. He also has a furniture restoration firm, and with his wife and partner, runs a highly successful business specializing in the manufacture of fine furniture for the private and professional decorator.

Davidson has contributed to a large number of publications on antique furniture, including Miller's *Understanding Antiques*.

GLASS

Mark West is a BADA (British Antiques Dealers Association) glass dealer based in Wimbledon in London. He has concentrated on glass collecting for more than 20 years and his shop carries an enormous range, particularly of 18th and 19th century English and continental glassware. He has contributed articles to various specialist publications.

SILVER & PLATE

John Wilson is an acclaimed silver expert and Freeman of the Goldsmith's Company, and has worked in the Silver Department at Sotheby's in London. Wilson's previous work for Miller's includes the section on silver and plate in the best-selling *Miller's Understanding Antiques*.

DOLLS & TEDDY BEARS

Sue Pearson has been a dealer and collector of antique dolls and teddy bears for many years. She has a shop in Brighton and also runs a doll and teddy bear hospital. Pearson also contributes to several teddy bear magazines.

CLOCKS

John Mighell is the owner of *Strike One*, which has specialized in the restoration and sale of antique clocks and barometers for the past 25 years. He has an extensive knowledge of English, Continental and American clocks, and is the author of numerous articles on clock collecting.

Mighell has played a leading role in bringing previously neglected areas of horology, such as tavern clocks and Vienna regulators, to the attention of clock collectors throughout the world.

POTTERY AND PORCELAIN

Gordon Lang has worked at Sotheby's for 21 years, and is the Senior Tutor and Director of their Postgraduate programme in Asian Arts run in conjunction with the School of Oriental and African Studies (SOAS) at the University of London.

Lang has contributed to many books on ceramics, including *Sotheby's Concise Encyclopedia of Porcelain* (Conran Octopus). He appears regularly on the popular BBC's *Antiques Roadshow* and lives in London.

SERIES CONSULTANTS

Judith and Martin Miller are internationally famous figures in the world of antiques. In 1979 they set up their own company to produce the annual *Miller's Antiques Price Guide*, the bible of the antiques trade. The price guide now has annual sales of over 135,000 copies worldwide.

In the wake of the success of the *Antiques Price Guide*, further best-selling price guides have been produced by Millers on pictures, collectables, cars and motorcycles.

MILLER'S ORDER FORM

TITLE	PRICE	QTY	TOTAL (£)
0855338881 Miller's Antiques Checklist Art Deco	£9.99		
0855339195 Miller's Antiques Checklist Art Nouveau	£9.99		
0855339195 Miller's Antiques Checklist Clocks	£9.99		
1857329456 Miller's Antiques Checklist Dolls & Teddy Bears	£9.99		
085533889x Miller's Antiques Checklist Furniture	£9.99		
0855338946 Miller's Antiques Checklist Porcelain	£9.99		
0855338954 Miller's Antiques Checklist Victoriana	£9.99		
185732272x Miller's Antiques Checklist Silver & Plate	£9.99		
1857322711 Miller's Antiques Checklist Glass	£9.99		
1857322738 Miller's Antiques Checklist Pottery	£9.99		
1857323416 Miller's Antiques Price Guide 1995	£19.99		
1857325427 Miller's Collectables Price Guide 1995/6	£16.99		
1857321790 Antiques & Collectables: The Facts at Your Fingertips	£7.99PB		
1857320018 Understanding Antiques	£14.99PB		
0855336897 Miller's Pocket Antiques Fact File	£6.99		
1857320964 Miller's Silver & Sheffield Plate Marks	£6.99		
	Total		
	P&P (see note)		
	Payment due		

Postage & Packing Charges
Please add £1.50 for all orders under £10.00.
Postage and packing is FREE for order of
£10.00 and over to UK, NI, BFPO. For
delivery outside the UK, please add £3.00 per order towards carriage.

All books are hardback unless otherwise shown. The prices were
correct at the time of going to press, but Miller's reserve the right
to increase prices at short notice.

How to order
Simply use the order form and return it to us with your credit card
details or a cheque/postal order made payable to Reed Book Services
or telephone the credit card hotline on 01933 414000.

Method of Payment
1. I attach a cheque or postal order to the value of £ ....
2. Please debit my ACCESS/VISA/AMEX/DINERS CARD (please
delete) by the amount shown.

NAME (Block letters)..

ADDRESS..

....POSTCODE........................

Card Number ☐☐☐☐☐☐☐☐☐☐☐☐☐☐☐☐

Expiry Date ☐☐☐☐

Signature ....

Send your completed form to:
Miller's Club, Reed Book Services Limited, PO Box 5, Rushden,
Northants NN10 6YX

All titles are subject to availability. Orders are normally despatched within 5 days, but
please allow up to 28 days for delivery.

If you do not wish your name to be used by other carefully selected
organisations for promotional purposes, please tick this box. ☐

Registered office: Michelin House, 81 Fulham Road, London SW3 6RB. Reg. in England
no. 1974080.